C-1646   CAREER EXAMINATION SERIES

This is your
PASSBOOK for...

School Secretary

Test Preparation Study Guide
Questions & Answers

COPYRIGHT NOTICE

This book is SOLELY intended for, is sold ONLY to, and its use is RESTRICTED to individual, bona fide applicants or candidates who qualify by virtue of having seriously filed applications for appropriate license, certificate, professional and/or promotional advancement, higher school matriculation, scholarship, or other legitimate requirements of education and/or governmental authorities.

This book is NOT intended for use, class instruction, tutoring, training, duplication, copying, reprinting, excerption, or adaptation, etc., by:

1) Other publishers
2) Proprietors and/or Instructors of "Coaching" and/or Preparatory Courses
3) Personnel and/or Training Divisions of commercial, industrial, and governmental organizations
4) Schools, colleges, or universities and/or their departments and staffs, including teachers and other personnel
5) Testing Agencies or Bureaus
6) Study groups which seek by the purchase of a single volume to copy and/or duplicate and/or adapt this material for use by the group as a whole without having purchased individual volumes for each of the members of the group
7) Et al.

Such persons would be in violation of appropriate Federal and State statutes.

PROVISION OF LICENSING AGREEMENTS – Recognized educational, commercial, industrial, and governmental institutions and organizations, and others legitimately engaged in educational pursuits, including training, testing, and measurement activities, may address request for a licensing agreement to the copyright owners, who will determine whether, and under what conditions, including fees and charges, the materials in this book may be used them. In other words, a licensing facility exists for the legitimate use of the material in this book on other than an individual basis. However, it is asseverated and affirmed here that the material in this book CANNOT be used without the receipt of the express permission of such a licensing agreement from the Publishers. Inquiries re licensing should be addressed to the company, attention rights and permissions department.

All rights reserved, including the right of reproduction in whole or in part, in any form or by any means, electronic or mechanical, including photocopying, recording, or by any information storage and retrieval system, without permission in writing from the Publisher.

Copyright © 2024 by
National Learning Corporation

212 Michael Drive, Syosset, NY 11791
(516) 921-8888 • www.passbooks.com
E-mail: info@passbooks.com

PASSBOOK® SERIES

THE *PASSBOOK® SERIES* has been created to prepare applicants and candidates for the ultimate academic battlefield – the examination room.

At some time in our lives, each and every one of us may be required to take an examination – for validation, matriculation, admission, qualification, registration, certification, or licensure.

Based on the assumption that every applicant or candidate has met the basic formal educational standards, has taken the required number of courses, and read the necessary texts, the *PASSBOOK® SERIES* furnishes the one special preparation which may assure passing with confidence, instead of failing with insecurity. Examination questions – together with answers – are furnished as the basic vehicle for study so that the mysteries of the examination and its compounding difficulties may be eliminated or diminished by a sure method.

This book is meant to help you pass your examination provided that you qualify and are serious in your objective.

The entire field is reviewed through the huge store of content information which is succinctly presented through a provocative and challenging approach – the question-and-answer method.

A climate of success is established by furnishing the correct answers at the end of each test.

You soon learn to recognize types of questions, forms of questions, and patterns of questioning. You may even begin to anticipate expected outcomes.

You perceive that many questions are repeated or adapted so that you can gain acute insights, which may enable you to score many sure points.

You learn how to confront new questions, or types of questions, and to attack them confidently and work out the correct answers.

You note objectives and emphases, and recognize pitfalls and dangers, so that you may make positive educational adjustments.

Moreover, you are kept fully informed in relation to new concepts, methods, practices, and directions in the field.

You discover that you are actually taking the examination all the time: you are preparing for the examination by "taking" an examination, not by reading extraneous and/or supererogatory textbooks.

In short, this PASSBOOK®, used directedly, should be an important factor in helping you to pass your test.

SCHOOL SECRETARY

DUTIES

Under general supervision, an incumbent of this position performs responsible and confidential work as an executive secretary to a high level school building or district-wide administrator, other than the chief school officer or school principal, such as an Assistant Superintendent. This position requires a full range of skill in the operation of computers in compiling and producing correspondence, reports, records, files, etc. The frequent use of independent judgment and discretion in screening callers and planning the routine of the office is required. Detailed instructions are received only upon work involving questions of policy determination and administration. Incumbents must be fluent in both the Spanish and English languages, providing interpretive and information services. This position is distinguished from the title of "Secretary-Stenographer" in that stenography is not required. It is distinguished from lower level titles such as Secretary (School Districts) and Senior Office Assistant (Automated Systems) by the level of the supervisor as well as the scope and complexity of the duties assigned. Supervision may be exercised over the work of lower level clerical support personnel. Does related work as required.

SCOPE OF THE EXAMINATION

The Written Test is designed to test for knowledge, skills, and/or abilities in such areas as:
1. Grammar/usage / punctuation;
2. Keyboarding practices;
3. Office record keeping;
4. Office practices;
5. Spelling; and
6. Principles of word processing.

HOW TO TAKE A TEST

I. YOU MUST PASS AN EXAMINATION

A. WHAT EVERY CANDIDATE SHOULD KNOW

Examination applicants often ask us for help in preparing for the written test. What can I study in advance? What kinds of questions will be asked? How will the test be given? How will the papers be graded?

As an applicant for a civil service examination, you may be wondering about some of these things. Our purpose here is to suggest effective methods of advance study and to describe civil service examinations.

Your chances for success on this examination can be increased if you know how to prepare. Those "pre-examination jitters" can be reduced if you know what to expect. You can even experience an adventure in good citizenship if you know why civil service exams are given.

B. WHY ARE CIVIL SERVICE EXAMINATIONS GIVEN?

Civil service examinations are important to you in two ways. As a citizen, you want public jobs filled by employees who know how to do their work. As a job seeker, you want a fair chance to compete for that job on an equal footing with other candidates. The best-known means of accomplishing this two-fold goal is the competitive examination.

Exams are widely publicized throughout the nation. They may be administered for jobs in federal, state, city, municipal, town or village governments or agencies.

Any citizen may apply, with some limitations, such as the age or residence of applicants. Your experience and education may be reviewed to see whether you meet the requirements for the particular examination. When these requirements exist, they are reasonable and applied consistently to all applicants. Thus, a competitive examination may cause you some uneasiness now, but it is your privilege and safeguard.

C. HOW ARE CIVIL SERVICE EXAMS DEVELOPED?

Examinations are carefully written by trained technicians who are specialists in the field known as "psychological measurement," in consultation with recognized authorities in the field of work that the test will cover. These experts recommend the subject matter areas or skills to be tested; only those knowledges or skills important to your success on the job are included. The most reliable books and source materials available are used as references. Together, the experts and technicians judge the difficulty level of the questions.

Test technicians know how to phrase questions so that the problem is clearly stated. Their ethics do not permit "trick" or "catch" questions. Questions may have been tried out on sample groups, or subjected to statistical analysis, to determine their usefulness.

Written tests are often used in combination with performance tests, ratings of training and experience, and oral interviews. All of these measures combine to form the best-known means of finding the right person for the right job.

II. HOW TO PASS THE WRITTEN TEST

A. NATURE OF THE EXAMINATION

To prepare intelligently for civil service examinations, you should know how they differ from school examinations you have taken. In school you were assigned certain definite pages to read or subjects to cover. The examination questions were quite detailed and usually emphasized memory. Civil service exams, on the other hand, try to discover your present ability to perform the duties of a position, plus your potentiality to learn these duties. In other words, a civil service exam attempts to predict how successful you will be. Questions cover such a broad area that they cannot be as minute and detailed as school exam questions.

In the public service similar kinds of work, or positions, are grouped together in one "class." This process is known as *position-classification*. All the positions in a class are paid according to the salary range for that class. One class title covers all of these positions, and they are all tested by the same examination.

B. FOUR BASIC STEPS

1) Study the announcement

How, then, can you know what subjects to study? Our best answer is: "Learn as much as possible about the class of positions for which you've applied." The exam will test the knowledge, skills and abilities needed to do the work.

Your most valuable source of information about the position you want is the official exam announcement. This announcement lists the training and experience qualifications. Check these standards and apply only if you come reasonably close to meeting them.

The brief description of the position in the examination announcement offers some clues to the subjects which will be tested. Think about the job itself. Review the duties in your mind. Can you perform them, or are there some in which you are rusty? Fill in the blank spots in your preparation.

Many jurisdictions preview the written test in the exam announcement by including a section called "Knowledge and Abilities Required," "Scope of the Examination," or some similar heading. Here you will find out specifically what fields will be tested.

2) Review your own background

Once you learn in general what the position is all about, and what you need to know to do the work, ask yourself which subjects you already know fairly well and which need improvement. You may wonder whether to concentrate on improving your strong areas or on building some background in your fields of weakness. When the announcement has specified "some knowledge" or "considerable knowledge," or has used adjectives like "beginning principles of…" or "advanced … methods," you can get a clue as to the number and difficulty of questions to be asked in any given field. More questions, and hence broader coverage, would be included for those subjects which are more important in the work. Now weigh your strengths and weaknesses against the job requirements and prepare accordingly.

3) Determine the level of the position

Another way to tell how intensively you should prepare is to understand the level of the job for which you are applying. Is it the entering level? In other words, is this the position in which beginners in a field of work are hired? Or is it an intermediate or advanced level? Sometimes this is indicated by such words as "Junior" or "Senior" in the class title. Other jurisdictions use Roman numerals to designate the level – Clerk I, Clerk II, for example. The word "Supervisor" sometimes appears in the title. If the level is not indicated by the title, check the description of duties. Will you be working under very close supervision, or will you have responsibility for independent decisions in this work?

4) Choose appropriate study materials

Now that you know the subjects to be examined and the relative amount of each subject to be covered, you can choose suitable study materials. For beginning level jobs, or even advanced ones, if you have a pronounced weakness in some aspect of your training, read a modern, standard textbook in that field. Be sure it is up to date and has general coverage. Such books are normally available at your library, and the librarian will be glad to help you locate one. For entry-level positions, questions of appropriate difficulty are chosen – neither highly advanced questions, nor those too simple. Such questions require careful thought but not advanced training.

If the position for which you are applying is technical or advanced, you will read more advanced, specialized material. If you are already familiar with the basic principles of your field, elementary textbooks would waste your time. Concentrate on advanced textbooks and technical periodicals. Think through the concepts and review difficult problems in your field.

These are all general sources. You can get more ideas on your own initiative, following these leads. For example, training manuals and publications of the government agency which employs workers in your field can be useful, particularly for technical and professional positions. A letter or visit to the government department involved may result in more specific study suggestions, and certainly will provide you with a more definite idea of the exact nature of the position you are seeking.

III. KINDS OF TESTS

Tests are used for purposes other than measuring knowledge and ability to perform specified duties. For some positions, it is equally important to test ability to make adjustments to new situations or to profit from training. In others, basic mental abilities not dependent on information are essential. Questions which test these things may not appear as pertinent to the duties of the position as those which test for knowledge and information. Yet they are often highly important parts of a fair examination. For very general questions, it is almost impossible to help you direct your study efforts. What we can do is to point out some of the more common of these general abilities needed in public service positions and describe some typical questions.

1) General information

Broad, general information has been found useful for predicting job success in some kinds of work. This is tested in a variety of ways, from vocabulary lists to questions about current events. Basic background in some field of work, such as sociology or economics, may be sampled in a group of questions. Often these are principles which have become familiar to most persons through exposure rather than through formal training. It is difficult to advise you how to study for these questions; being alert to the world around you is our best suggestion.

2) Verbal ability

An example of an ability needed in many positions is verbal or language ability. Verbal ability is, in brief, the ability to use and understand words. Vocabulary and grammar tests are typical measures of this ability. Reading comprehension or paragraph interpretation questions are common in many kinds of civil service tests. You are given a paragraph of written material and asked to find its central meaning.

3) Numerical ability

Number skills can be tested by the familiar arithmetic problem, by checking paired lists of numbers to see which are alike and which are different, or by interpreting charts and graphs. In the latter test, a graph may be printed in the test booklet which you are asked to use as the basis for answering questions.

4) Observation

A popular test for law-enforcement positions is the observation test. A picture is shown to you for several minutes, then taken away. Questions about the picture test your ability to observe both details and larger elements.

5) Following directions

In many positions in the public service, the employee must be able to carry out written instructions dependably and accurately. You may be given a chart with several columns, each column listing a variety of information. The questions require you to carry out directions involving the information given in the chart.

6) Skills and aptitudes

Performance tests effectively measure some manual skills and aptitudes. When the skill is one in which you are trained, such as typing or shorthand, you can practice. These tests are often very much like those given in business school or high school courses. For many of the other skills and aptitudes, however, no short-time preparation can be made. Skills and abilities natural to you or that you have developed throughout your lifetime are being tested.

Many of the general questions just described provide all the data needed to answer the questions and ask you to use your reasoning ability to find the answers. Your best preparation for these tests, as well as for tests of facts and ideas, is to be at your physical and mental best. You, no doubt, have your own methods of getting into an exam-taking mood and keeping "in shape." The next section lists some ideas on this subject.

IV. KINDS OF QUESTIONS

Only rarely is the "essay" question, which you answer in narrative form, used in civil service tests. Civil service tests are usually of the short-answer type. Full instructions for answering these questions will be given to you at the examination. But in case this is your first experience with short-answer questions and separate answer sheets, here is what you need to know:

1) **Multiple-choice Questions**

Most popular of the short-answer questions is the "multiple choice" or "best answer" question. It can be used, for example, to test for factual knowledge, ability to solve problems or judgment in meeting situations found at work.

A multiple-choice question is normally one of three types—
- It can begin with an incomplete statement followed by several possible endings. You are to find the one ending which *best* completes the statement, although some of the others may not be entirely wrong.
- It can also be a complete statement in the form of a question which is answered by choosing one of the statements listed.

- It can be in the form of a problem – again you select the best answer.

Here is an example of a multiple-choice question with a discussion which should give you some clues as to the method for choosing the right answer:

When an employee has a complaint about his assignment, the action which will *best* help him overcome his difficulty is to
   A. discuss his difficulty with his coworkers
   B. take the problem to the head of the organization
   C. take the problem to the person who gave him the assignment
   D. say nothing to anyone about his complaint

In answering this question, you should study each of the choices to find which is best. Consider choice "A" – Certainly an employee may discuss his complaint with fellow employees, but no change or improvement can result, and the complaint remains unresolved. Choice "B" is a poor choice since the head of the organization probably does not know what assignment you have been given, and taking your problem to him is known as "going over the head" of the supervisor. The supervisor, or person who made the assignment, is the person who can clarify it or correct any injustice. Choice "C" is, therefore, correct. To say nothing, as in choice "D," is unwise. Supervisors have and interest in knowing the problems employees are facing, and the employee is seeking a solution to his problem.

2) True/False Questions

The "true/false" or "right/wrong" form of question is sometimes used. Here a complete statement is given. Your job is to decide whether the statement is right or wrong.

SAMPLE: A roaming cell-phone call to a nearby city costs less than a non-roaming call to a distant city.

This statement is wrong, or false, since roaming calls are more expensive.

This is not a complete list of all possible question forms, although most of the others are variations of these common types. You will always get complete directions for answering questions. Be sure you understand *how* to mark your answers – ask questions until you do.

V. RECORDING YOUR ANSWERS

Computer terminals are used more and more today for many different kinds of exams.
For an examination with very few applicants, you may be told to record your answers in the test booklet itself. Separate answer sheets are much more common. If this separate answer sheet is to be scored by machine – and this is often the case – it is highly important that you mark your answers correctly in order to get credit.
An electronic scoring machine is often used in civil service offices because of the speed with which papers can be scored. Machine-scored answer sheets must be marked with a pencil, which will be given to you. This pencil has a high graphite content which responds to the electronic scoring machine. As a matter of fact, stray dots may register as answers, so do not let your pencil rest on the answer sheet while you are pondering the correct answer. Also, if your pencil lead breaks or is otherwise defective, ask for another.

Since the answer sheet will be dropped in a slot in the scoring machine, be careful not to bend the corners or get the paper crumpled.

The answer sheet normally has five vertical columns of numbers, with 30 numbers to a column. These numbers correspond to the question numbers in your test booklet. After each number, going across the page are four or five pairs of dotted lines. These short dotted lines have small letters or numbers above them. The first two pairs may also have a "T" or "F" above the letters. This indicates that the first two pairs only are to be used if the questions are of the true-false type. If the questions are multiple choice, disregard the "T" and "F" and pay attention only to the small letters or numbers.

Answer your questions in the manner of the sample that follows:

32. The largest city in the United States is
    A. Washington, D.C.
    B. New York City
    C. Chicago
    D. Detroit
    E. San Francisco

1) Choose the answer you think is best. (New York City is the largest, so "B" is correct.)
2) Find the row of dotted lines numbered the same as the question you are answering. (Find row number 32)
3) Find the pair of dotted lines corresponding to the answer. (Find the pair of lines under the mark "B.")
4) Make a solid black mark between the dotted lines.

VI. BEFORE THE TEST

Common sense will help you find procedures to follow to get ready for an examination. Too many of us, however, overlook these sensible measures. Indeed, nervousness and fatigue have been found to be the most serious reasons why applicants fail to do their best on civil service tests. Here is a list of reminders:

- Begin your preparation early – Don't wait until the last minute to go scurrying around for books and materials or to find out what the position is all about.
- Prepare continuously – An hour a night for a week is better than an all-night cram session. This has been definitely established. What is more, a night a week for a month will return better dividends than crowding your study into a shorter period of time.
- Locate the place of the exam – You have been sent a notice telling you when and where to report for the examination. If the location is in a different town or otherwise unfamiliar to you, it would be well to inquire the best route and learn something about the building.
- Relax the night before the test – Allow your mind to rest. Do not study at all that night. Plan some mild recreation or diversion; then go to bed early and get a good night's sleep.
- Get up early enough to make a leisurely trip to the place for the test – This way unforeseen events, traffic snarls, unfamiliar buildings, etc. will not upset you.
- Dress comfortably – A written test is not a fashion show. You will be known by number and not by name, so wear something comfortable.

- Leave excess paraphernalia at home – Shopping bags and odd bundles will get in your way. You need bring only the items mentioned in the official notice you received; usually everything you need is provided. Do not bring reference books to the exam. They will only confuse those last minutes and be taken away from you when in the test room.
- Arrive somewhat ahead of time – If because of transportation schedules you must get there very early, bring a newspaper or magazine to take your mind off yourself while waiting.
- Locate the examination room – When you have found the proper room, you will be directed to the seat or part of the room where you will sit. Sometimes you are given a sheet of instructions to read while you are waiting. Do not fill out any forms until you are told to do so; just read them and be prepared.
- Relax and prepare to listen to the instructions
- If you have any physical problem that may keep you from doing your best, be sure to tell the test administrator. If you are sick or in poor health, you really cannot do your best on the exam. You can come back and take the test some other time.

VII. AT THE TEST

The day of the test is here and you have the test booklet in your hand. The temptation to get going is very strong. Caution! There is more to success than knowing the right answers. You must know how to identify your papers and understand variations in the type of short-answer question used in this particular examination. Follow these suggestions for maximum results from your efforts:

1) Cooperate with the monitor

The test administrator has a duty to create a situation in which you can be as much at ease as possible. He will give instructions, tell you when to begin, check to see that you are marking your answer sheet correctly, and so on. He is not there to guard you, although he will see that your competitors do not take unfair advantage. He wants to help you do your best.

2) Listen to all instructions

Don't jump the gun! Wait until you understand all directions. In most civil service tests you get more time than you need to answer the questions. So don't be in a hurry. Read each word of instructions until you clearly understand the meaning. Study the examples, listen to all announcements and follow directions. Ask questions if you do not understand what to do.

3) Identify your papers

Civil service exams are usually identified by number only. You will be assigned a number; you must not put your name on your test papers. Be sure to copy your number correctly. Since more than one exam may be given, copy your exact examination title.

4) Plan your time

Unless you are told that a test is a "speed" or "rate of work" test, speed itself is usually not important. Time enough to answer all the questions will be provided, but this does not mean that you have all day. An overall time limit has been set. Divide the total time (in minutes) by the number of questions to determine the approximate time you have for each question.

5) Do not linger over difficult questions

If you come across a difficult question, mark it with a paper clip (useful to have along) and come back to it when you have been through the booklet. One caution if you do this – be sure to skip a number on your answer sheet as well. Check often to be sure that you have not lost your place and that you are marking in the row numbered the same as the question you are answering.

6) Read the questions

Be sure you know what the question asks! Many capable people are unsuccessful because they failed to *read* the questions correctly.

7) Answer all questions

Unless you have been instructed that a penalty will be deducted for incorrect answers, it is better to guess than to omit a question.

8) Speed tests

It is often better NOT to guess on speed tests. It has been found that on timed tests people are tempted to spend the last few seconds before time is called in marking answers at random – without even reading them – in the hope of picking up a few extra points. To discourage this practice, the instructions may warn you that your score will be "corrected" for guessing. That is, a penalty will be applied. The incorrect answers will be deducted from the correct ones, or some other penalty formula will be used.

9) Review your answers

If you finish before time is called, go back to the questions you guessed or omitted to give them further thought. Review other answers if you have time.

10) Return your test materials

If you are ready to leave before others have finished or time is called, take ALL your materials to the monitor and leave quietly. Never take any test material with you. The monitor can discover whose papers are not complete, and taking a test booklet may be grounds for disqualification.

VIII. EXAMINATION TECHNIQUES

1) Read the general instructions carefully. These are usually printed on the first page of the exam booklet. As a rule, these instructions refer to the timing of the examination; the fact that you should not start work until the signal and must stop work at a signal, etc. If there are any *special* instructions, such as a choice of questions to be answered, make sure that you note this instruction carefully.

2) When you are ready to start work on the examination, that is as soon as the signal has been given, read the instructions to each question booklet, underline any key words or phrases, such as *least, best, outline, describe* and the like. In this way you will tend to answer as requested rather than discover on reviewing your paper that you *listed without describing*, that you selected the *worst* choice rather than the *best* choice, etc.

3) If the examination is of the objective or multiple-choice type – that is, each question will also give a series of possible answers: A, B, C or D, and you are called upon to select the best answer and write the letter next to that answer on your answer paper – it is advisable to start answering each question in turn. There may be anywhere from 50 to 100 such questions in the three or four hours allotted and you can see how much time would be taken if you read through all the questions before beginning to answer any. Furthermore, if you come across a question or group of questions which you know would be difficult to answer, it would undoubtedly affect your handling of all the other questions.

4) If the examination is of the essay type and contains but a few questions, it is a moot point as to whether you should read all the questions before starting to answer any one. Of course, if you are given a choice – say five out of seven and the like – then it is essential to read all the questions so you can eliminate the two that are most difficult. If, however, you are asked to answer all the questions, there may be danger in trying to answer the easiest one first because you may find that you will spend too much time on it. The best technique is to answer the first question, then proceed to the second, etc.

5) Time your answers. Before the exam begins, write down the time it started, then add the time allowed for the examination and write down the time it must be completed, then divide the time available somewhat as follows:
    - If 3-1/2 hours are allowed, that would be 210 minutes. If you have 80 objective-type questions, that would be an average of 2-1/2 minutes per question. Allow yourself no more than 2 minutes per question, or a total of 160 minutes, which will permit about 50 minutes to review.
    - If for the time allotment of 210 minutes there are 7 essay questions to answer, that would average about 30 minutes a question. Give yourself only 25 minutes per question so that you have about 35 minutes to review.

6) The most important instruction is to *read each question* and make sure you know what is wanted. The second most important instruction is to *time yourself properly* so that you answer every question. The third most important instruction is to *answer every question*. Guess if you have to but include something for each question. Remember that you will receive no credit for a blank and will probably receive some credit if you write something in answer to an essay question. If you guess a letter – say "B" for a multiple-choice question – you may have guessed right. If you leave a blank as an answer to a multiple-choice question, the examiners may respect your feelings but it will not add a point to your score. Some exams may penalize you for wrong answers, so in such cases *only*, you may not want to guess unless you have some basis for your answer.

7) Suggestions
    a. Objective-type questions
        1. Examine the question booklet for proper sequence of pages and questions
        2. Read all instructions carefully
        3. Skip any question which seems too difficult; return to it after all other questions have been answered
        4. Apportion your time properly; do not spend too much time on any single question or group of questions

5. Note and underline key words – *all, most, fewest, least, best, worst, same, opposite,* etc.
6. Pay particular attention to negatives
7. Note unusual option, e.g., unduly long, short, complex, different or similar in content to the body of the question
8. Observe the use of "hedging" words – *probably, may, most likely,* etc.
9. Make sure that your answer is put next to the same number as the question
10. Do not second-guess unless you have good reason to believe the second answer is definitely more correct
11. Cross out original answer if you decide another answer is more accurate; do not erase until you are ready to hand your paper in
12. Answer all questions; guess unless instructed otherwise
13. Leave time for review

  b. Essay questions
   1. Read each question carefully
   2. Determine exactly what is wanted. Underline key words or phrases.
   3. Decide on outline or paragraph answer
   4. Include many different points and elements unless asked to develop any one or two points or elements
   5. Show impartiality by giving pros and cons unless directed to select one side only
   6. Make and write down any assumptions you find necessary to answer the questions
   7. Watch your English, grammar, punctuation and choice of words
   8. Time your answers; don't crowd material

8) Answering the essay question

Most essay questions can be answered by framing the specific response around several key words or ideas. Here are a few such key words or ideas:

M's: manpower, materials, methods, money, management
P's: purpose, program, policy, plan, procedure, practice, problems, pitfalls, personnel, public relations

  a. Six basic steps in handling problems:
   1. Preliminary plan and background development
   2. Collect information, data and facts
   3. Analyze and interpret information, data and facts
   4. Analyze and develop solutions as well as make recommendations
   5. Prepare report and sell recommendations
   6. Install recommendations and follow up effectiveness

  b. Pitfalls to avoid
   1. *Taking things for granted* – A statement of the situation does not necessarily imply that each of the elements is necessarily true; for example, a complaint may be invalid and biased so that all that can be taken for granted is that a complaint has been registered

2. *Considering only one side of a situation* – Wherever possible, indicate several alternatives and then point out the reasons you selected the best one
3. *Failing to indicate follow up* – Whenever your answer indicates action on your part, make certain that you will take proper follow-up action to see how successful your recommendations, procedures or actions turn out to be
4. *Taking too long in answering any single question* – Remember to time your answers properly

IX. AFTER THE TEST

Scoring procedures differ in detail among civil service jurisdictions although the general principles are the same. Whether the papers are hand-scored or graded by machine we have described, they are nearly always graded by number. That is, the person who marks the paper knows only the number – never the name – of the applicant. Not until all the papers have been graded will they be matched with names. If other tests, such as training and experience or oral interview ratings have been given, scores will be combined. Different parts of the examination usually have different weights. For example, the written test might count 60 percent of the final grade, and a rating of training and experience 40 percent. In many jurisdictions, veterans will have a certain number of points added to their grades.

After the final grade has been determined, the names are placed in grade order and an eligible list is established. There are various methods for resolving ties between those who get the same final grade – probably the most common is to place first the name of the person whose application was received first. Job offers are made from the eligible list in the order the names appear on it. You will be notified of your grade and your rank as soon as all these computations have been made. This will be done as rapidly as possible.

People who are found to meet the requirements in the announcement are called "eligibles." Their names are put on a list of eligible candidates. An eligible's chances of getting a job depend on how high he stands on this list and how fast agencies are filling jobs from the list.

When a job is to be filled from a list of eligibles, the agency asks for the names of people on the list of eligibles for that job. When the civil service commission receives this request, it sends to the agency the names of the three people highest on this list. Or, if the job to be filled has specialized requirements, the office sends the agency the names of the top three persons who meet these requirements from the general list.

The appointing officer makes a choice from among the three people whose names were sent to him. If the selected person accepts the appointment, the names of the others are put back on the list to be considered for future openings.

That is the rule in hiring from all kinds of eligible lists, whether they are for typist, carpenter, chemist, or something else. For every vacancy, the appointing officer has his choice of any one of the top three eligibles on the list. This explains why the person whose name is on top of the list sometimes does not get an appointment when some of the persons lower on the list do. If the appointing officer chooses the second or third eligible, the No. 1 eligible does not get a job at once, but stays on the list until he is appointed or the list is terminated.

X. HOW TO PASS THE INTERVIEW TEST

The examination for which you applied requires an oral interview test. You have already taken the written test and you are now being called for the interview test – the final part of the formal examination.

You may think that it is not possible to prepare for an interview test and that there are no procedures to follow during an interview. Our purpose is to point out some things you can do in advance that will help you and some good rules to follow and pitfalls to avoid while you are being interviewed.

What is an interview supposed to test?

The written examination is designed to test the technical knowledge and competence of the candidate; the oral is designed to evaluate intangible qualities, not readily measured otherwise, and to establish a list showing the relative fitness of each candidate – as measured against his competitors – for the position sought. Scoring is not on the basis of "right" and "wrong," but on a sliding scale of values ranging from "not passable" to "outstanding." As a matter of fact, it is possible to achieve a relatively low score without a single "incorrect" answer because of evident weakness in the qualities being measured.

Occasionally, an examination may consist entirely of an oral test – either an individual or a group oral. In such cases, information is sought concerning the technical knowledges and abilities of the candidate, since there has been no written examination for this purpose. More commonly, however, an oral test is used to supplement a written examination.

Who conducts interviews?

The composition of oral boards varies among different jurisdictions. In nearly all, a representative of the personnel department serves as chairman. One of the members of the board may be a representative of the department in which the candidate would work. In some cases, "outside experts" are used, and, frequently, a businessman or some other representative of the general public is asked to serve. Labor and management or other special groups may be represented. The aim is to secure the services of experts in the appropriate field.

However the board is composed, it is a good idea (and not at all improper or unethical) to ascertain in advance of the interview who the members are and what groups they represent. When you are introduced to them, you will have some idea of their backgrounds and interests, and at least you will not stutter and stammer over their names.

What should be done before the interview?

While knowledge about the board members is useful and takes some of the surprise element out of the interview, there is other preparation which is more substantive. It *is* possible to prepare for an oral interview – in several ways:

1) Keep a copy of your application and review it carefully before the interview

This may be the only document before the oral board, and the starting point of the interview. Know what education and experience you have listed there, and the sequence and dates of all of it. Sometimes the board will ask you to review the highlights of your experience for them; you should not have to hem and haw doing it.

2) Study the class specification and the examination announcement

Usually, the oral board has one or both of these to guide them. The qualities, characteristics or knowledges required by the position sought are stated in these documents. They offer valuable clues as to the nature of the oral interview. For example, if the job involves supervisory responsibilities, the announcement will usually indicate that knowledge of modern supervisory methods and the qualifications of the candidate as a supervisor will be tested. If so, you can expect such questions, frequently in the form of a hypothetical situation which you are expected to solve. NEVER go into an oral without knowledge of the duties and responsibilities of the job you seek.

3) Think through each qualification required

Try to visualize the kind of questions you would ask if you were a board member. How well could you answer them? Try especially to appraise your own knowledge and background in each area, *measured against the job sought*, and identify any areas in which you are weak. Be critical and realistic – do not flatter yourself.

4) Do some general reading in areas in which you feel you may be weak

For example, if the job involves supervision and your past experience has NOT, some general reading in supervisory methods and practices, particularly in the field of human relations, might be useful. Do NOT study agency procedures or detailed manuals. The oral board will be testing your understanding and capacity, not your memory.

5) Get a good night's sleep and watch your general health and mental attitude

You will want a clear head at the interview. Take care of a cold or any other minor ailment, and of course, no hangovers.

What should be done on the day of the interview?

Now comes the day of the interview itself. Give yourself plenty of time to get there. Plan to arrive somewhat ahead of the scheduled time, particularly if your appointment is in the fore part of the day. If a previous candidate fails to appear, the board might be ready for you a bit early. By early afternoon an oral board is almost invariably behind schedule if there are many candidates, and you may have to wait. Take along a book or magazine to read, or your application to review, but leave any extraneous material in the waiting room when you go in for your interview. In any event, relax and compose yourself.

The matter of dress is important. The board is forming impressions about you – from your experience, your manners, your attitude, and your appearance. Give your personal appearance careful attention. Dress your best, but not your flashiest. Choose conservative, appropriate clothing, and be sure it is immaculate. This is a business interview, and your appearance should indicate that you regard it as such. Besides, being well groomed and properly dressed will help boost your confidence.

Sooner or later, someone will call your name and escort you into the interview room. *This is it.* From here on you are on your own. It is too late for any more preparation. But remember, you asked for this opportunity to prove your fitness, and you are here because your request was granted.

What happens when you go in?

The usual sequence of events will be as follows: The clerk (who is often the board stenographer) will introduce you to the chairman of the oral board, who will introduce you to the other members of the board. Acknowledge the introductions before you sit down. Do not be surprised if you find a microphone facing you or a stenotypist sitting by. Oral interviews are usually recorded in the event of an appeal or other review.

Usually the chairman of the board will open the interview by reviewing the highlights of your education and work experience from your application – primarily for the benefit of the other members of the board, as well as to get the material into the record. Do not interrupt or comment unless there is an error or significant misinterpretation; if that is the case, do not hesitate. But do not quibble about insignificant matters. Also, he will usually ask you some question about your education, experience or your present job – partly to get you to start talking and to establish the interviewing "rapport." He may start the actual questioning, or turn it over to one of the other members. Frequently, each member undertakes the questioning on a particular area, one in which he is perhaps most competent, so you can expect each member to participate in the examination. Because time is limited, you may also expect some rather abrupt switches in the direction the questioning takes, so do not be upset by it. Normally, a board member will not pursue a single line of questioning unless he discovers a particular strength or weakness.

After each member has participated, the chairman will usually ask whether any member has any further questions, then will ask you if you have anything you wish to add. Unless you are expecting this question, it may floor you. Worse, it may start you off on an extended, extemporaneous speech. The board is not usually seeking more information. The question is principally to offer you a last opportunity to present further qualifications or to indicate that you have nothing to add. So, if you feel that a significant qualification or characteristic has been overlooked, it is proper to point it out in a sentence or so. Do not compliment the board on the thoroughness of their examination – they have been sketchy, and you know it. If you wish, merely say, "No thank you, I have nothing further to add." This is a point where you can "talk yourself out" of a good impression or fail to present an important bit of information. Remember, *you close the interview yourself*.

The chairman will then say, "That is all, Mr. _____, thank you." Do not be startled; the interview is over, and quicker than you think. Thank him, gather your belongings and take your leave. Save your sigh of relief for the other side of the door.

How to put your best foot forward

Throughout this entire process, you may feel that the board individually and collectively is trying to pierce your defenses, seek out your hidden weaknesses and embarrass and confuse you. Actually, this is not true. They are obliged to make an appraisal of your qualifications for the job you are seeking, and they want to see you in your best light. Remember, they must interview all candidates and a non-cooperative candidate may become a failure in spite of their best efforts to bring out his qualifications. Here are 15 suggestions that will help you:

1) Be natural – Keep your attitude confident, not cocky

If you are not confident that you can do the job, do not expect the board to be. Do not apologize for your weaknesses, try to bring out your strong points. The board is interested in a positive, not negative, presentation. Cockiness will antagonize any board member and make him wonder if you are covering up a weakness by a false show of strength.

2) Get comfortable, but don't lounge or sprawl

Sit erectly but not stiffly. A careless posture may lead the board to conclude that you are careless in other things, or at least that you are not impressed by the importance of the occasion. Either conclusion is natural, even if incorrect. Do not fuss with your clothing, a pencil or an ashtray. Your hands may occasionally be useful to emphasize a point; do not let them become a point of distraction.

3) Do not wisecrack or make small talk

This is a serious situation, and your attitude should show that you consider it as such. Further, the time of the board is limited – they do not want to waste it, and neither should you.

4) Do not exaggerate your experience or abilities

In the first place, from information in the application or other interviews and sources, the board may know more about you than you think. Secondly, you probably will not get away with it. An experienced board is rather adept at spotting such a situation, so do not take the chance.

5) If you know a board member, do not make a point of it, yet do not hide it

Certainly you are not fooling him, and probably not the other members of the board. Do not try to take advantage of your acquaintanceship – it will probably do you little good.

6) Do not dominate the interview

Let the board do that. They will give you the clues – do not assume that you have to do all the talking. Realize that the board has a number of questions to ask you, and do not try to take up all the interview time by showing off your extensive knowledge of the answer to the first one.

7) Be attentive

You only have 20 minutes or so, and you should keep your attention at its sharpest throughout. When a member is addressing a problem or question to you, give him your undivided attention. Address your reply principally to him, but do not exclude the other board members.

8) Do not interrupt

A board member may be stating a problem for you to analyze. He will ask you a question when the time comes. Let him state the problem, and wait for the question.

9) Make sure you understand the question

Do not try to answer until you are sure what the question is. If it is not clear, restate it in your own words or ask the board member to clarify it for you. However, do not haggle about minor elements.

10) Reply promptly but not hastily

A common entry on oral board rating sheets is "candidate responded readily," or "candidate hesitated in replies." Respond as promptly and quickly as you can, but do not jump to a hasty, ill-considered answer.

11) Do not be peremptory in your answers

A brief answer is proper – but do not fire your answer back. That is a losing game from your point of view. The board member can probably ask questions much faster than you can answer them.

12) Do not try to create the answer you think the board member wants

He is interested in what kind of mind you have and how it works – not in playing games. Furthermore, he can usually spot this practice and will actually grade you down on it.

13) Do not switch sides in your reply merely to agree with a board member

Frequently, a member will take a contrary position merely to draw you out and to see if you are willing and able to defend your point of view. Do not start a debate, yet do not surrender a good position. If a position is worth taking, it is worth defending.

14) Do not be afraid to admit an error in judgment if you are shown to be wrong

The board knows that you are forced to reply without any opportunity for careful consideration. Your answer may be demonstrably wrong. If so, admit it and get on with the interview.

15) Do not dwell at length on your present job

The opening question may relate to your present assignment. Answer the question but do not go into an extended discussion. You are being examined for a *new* job, not your present one. As a matter of fact, try to phrase ALL your answers in terms of the job for which you are being examined.

Basis of Rating

Probably you will forget most of these "do's" and "don'ts" when you walk into the oral interview room. Even remembering them all will not ensure you a passing grade. Perhaps you did not have the qualifications in the first place. But remembering them will help you to put your best foot forward, without treading on the toes of the board members.

Rumor and popular opinion to the contrary notwithstanding, an oral board wants you to make the best appearance possible. They know you are under pressure – but they also want to see how you respond to it as a guide to what your reaction would be under the pressures of the job you seek. They will be influenced by the degree of poise you display, the personal traits you show and the manner in which you respond.

ABOUT THIS BOOK

This book contains tests divided into Examination Sections. Go through each test, answering every question in the margin. We have also attached a sample answer sheet at the back of the book that can be removed and used. At the end of each test look at the answer key and check your answers. On the ones you got wrong, look at the right answer choice and learn. Do not fill in the answers first. Do not memorize the questions and answers, but understand the answer and principles involved. On your test, the questions will likely be different from the samples. Questions are changed and new ones added. If you understand these past questions you should have success with any changes that arise. Tests may consist of several types of questions. We have additional books on each subject should more study be advisable or necessary for you. Finally, the more you study, the better prepared you will be. This book is intended to be the last thing you study before you walk into the examination room. Prior study of relevant texts is also recommended. NLC publishes some of these in our Fundamental Series. Knowledge and good sense are important factors in passing your exam. Good luck also helps. So now study this Passbook, absorb the material contained within and take that knowledge into the examination. Then do your best to pass that exam.

EXAMINATION SECTION

EXAMINATION SECTION

TEST 1

DIRECTIONS: Each question or incomplete statement is followed by several suggested answers or completions. Select the one that BEST answers the question or completes the statement. *PRINT THE LETTER OF THE CORRECT ANSWER IN THE SPACE AT THE RIGHT.*

1. The one of the following that is MOST advisable to do before transcribing your dictation notes is to
    A. check the syllabification of long words for typing purposes
    B. edit your notes
    C. number the pages of dictation
    D. sort them by the kind of typing format required

1._____

2. As a secretary, the one of the following which is LEAST important in writing a letter under your own signature is
    A. the accuracy of the information
    B. the appropriateness of the language
    C. the reason for the letter
    D. your supervisor's approval of the final copy

2._____

3. In a typed letter, the reference line is used
    A. for identification purposes on typed pages of more than one page
    B. to indicate under what heading the copy of the letter should be filed
    C. to indicate who dictated the letter and who typed it
    D. to make the subject of the letter prominent by typing it a single space below the salutation

3._____

Questions 4-5:

DIRECTIONS: For questions 4 and 5, choose the letter of the sentence that BEST and MOST clearly expresses its meaning.

4. A. It has always been the practice of this office to effectuate recruitment of prospective employees from other departments.
    B. This office has always made a practice of recruiting prospective employees from other departments.
    C. Recruitment of prospective employees from other departments has always been a practice which has been implemented by this office.
    D. Implementation of the policy of recruitment of prospective employees from other departments has always been a practice of this office.

4._____

5. A. These employees are assigned to the level of work evidenced by their efforts and skills during the training period.
    B. The level of work to which these employees is assigned is decided upon on the basis of the efforts and skills evidenced by them during the period in which they were trained.
    C. Assignment of these employees is made on the basis of the level of work their efforts and skills during the training period has evidenced.
    D. These employees are assigned to a level of work their efforts and skills during the training period have evidenced.

6. An office assistant was asked to mail a duplicated report of 100 pages to a professor in an out-of-town university. The professor sending the report dictated a short letter that he wanted to mail with the report.
    Of the following, the MOST inexpensive proper means of sending these two items would be to send the report
    A. and the letter first class
    B. by parcel post and the letter separately by air mail
    C. and the letter by parcel post
    D. by parcel post and attach to the package an envelope with first-class postage in which is enclosed the letter

7. Plans are underway to determine the productivity of the typists who work in a central office. Of the procedures listed, the one generally considered the MOST accurate for finding out the typists' output is to
    A. keep a record of how much typing is done over specified periods of time
    B. ask each typist how fast she types when she is doing a great deal of word processing
    C. give each typist a timed test during a specified period
    D. ask the supervisor to estimate the typing speed of each subordinate

8. Assume that an executive regularly receives the four types of mail listed below.
    As a general rule, the executive's secretary should arrange the mail from top to bottom so that the top items are
    A. advertisements
    B. airmail letters
    C. business letters
    D. unopened personal letters

9. An office assistant in transcribing reports and letters from dictation should MOST generally assume that
    A. the transcript should be exactly what was dictated so there is little need to check any details
    B. the dictated material is merely an idea of what the dictator wanted to say so changes should be made to improve any part of the dictation
    C. there may be some slight changes, but essentially the transcription is to be a faithful copy of what was dictated
    D. the transcript is merely a very rough draft and should be typed quickly so that the dictator can review it and make changes preliminary to having the final copy typed

10. The one of the following which generally is the CHIEF disadvantage of using office machines in place of human workers in office work is that the machines are
    A. slower
    B. less accurate
    C. more costly
    D. less flexible

11. An office assistant in a New York City college is asked to place a call to a prospective visiting professor in Los Angeles. It is 1 p.m. in New York (EST). The time in Los Angeles is
    A. 9 a.m.   B. 10 a.m.   C. 4 p.m.   D. 5 p.m.

12. An office assistant is instructed to send a copy of a report to a professor located in a building across campus. The fastest and most efficient way for this report to reach the professor is by
    A. sending a messenger to hand-deliver it to the professor's office
    B. sending it via fax to the main office of the professor's department
    C. e-mailing it to the professor
    D. dictating the contents of the report to the professor over the phone

13. An office assistant is in the process of typing the forms for recommendation for promotion for a member of the faculty who is away for a week. She notes that two books of which he is the author are listed without dates.
    Of the following, the procedure she should BEST follow at this point generally is to
    A. postpone doing the job until the professor returns to campus the following week
    B. type the material omitting the books
    C. check the professor's office for copies of the books and obtain the correct data
    D. call the professor's wife and ask her when the books were published

14. An office has introduced work standards for all of the employees.
Of the following, it is MOST likely that use of such standards would tend to
    A. make it more difficult to determine numbers of employees needed
    B. lead to a substantial drop in morale among all of the employees
    C. reduce the possibility of planning to meet emergencies
    D. reduce uncertainty about the costs of doing tasks

15. Of the following clerical errors, the one which probably is LEAST important is
    A. adding 543 instead of 548 to a bookkeeping account
    B. putting the wrong code on a data processing card
    C. recording a transaction on the record of Henry Smith instead of on the record of Harry Smith
    D. writing John Murpfy instead of John Murphy when addressing an envelope

16. Of the following errors, the one which probably is MOST important is
    A. writing "they're" instead of "their" in an office memo
    B. misplacing a decimal point on a sales invoice
    C. forgetting to write the date on a note for a supervisor
    D. sending an e-mail to a misspelled e-mail address

17. The chairman of an academic department tells an office assistant that a meeting of the faculty is to be held four weeks from the current date.
Of the following responsibilities, the office assistant is MOST frequently held responsible for
    A. planning the agenda of the meeting
    B. presiding over the conduct of the meeting
    C. reserving the meeting room and notifying the members
    D. initiating all formal resolutions

18. Of the following, a centralized filing system is LEAST suitable for filing
    A. material which is confidential in nature
    B. routine correspondence
    C. periodic reports of the divisions of the department
    D. material used by several divisions of the department

19. A misplaced record is a lost record.
Of the following, the MOST valid implication of this statement in regard to office work is that
    A. all records in an office should be filed in strict alphabetical order
    B. accuracy in filing is essential
    C. only one method of filing should be used throughout the office
    D. files should be locked when not in use

20. When typing names or titles on a roll of folder labels, the one of the following which is MOST important to do is to type the caption
    A. as it appears on the papers to be placed in the folder
    B. in capital letters
    C. in exact indexing or filing order
    D. so that it appears near the bottom of the folder tab when the label is attached

20._____

21. A professor at a Boston university asks an office assistant to place a call to a fellow professor in San Francisco. The MOST appropriate local time for the assistant to place the call to the professor in California, given the time difference, would be
    A. 8:30 a.m.   B. 10:00 a.m.   C. 11:30 a.m.   D. 1:30 p.m.

21._____

22. When typing the rough draft of a report, the computer application you would use is
    A. Excel   B. Word
    C. PowerPoint   D. Internet Explorer

22._____

23. Which of the following is the BEST and most appropriate way to proofread and edit a report before submitting it to a supervisor for review?
    A. Scan the report with the program's spell check feature
    B. Proof the report yourself, then ask another office assistant to read the report over as well until it is finished
    C. Give the report to another office assistant who is more skilled at proofreading
    D. Use the spell checker, then scan the report yourself as many times as needed in order to pick up any additional errors

23._____

24. The one of the following situations in which it would be MOST justifiable for an office to use standard or form paragraphs in its business letters is when
    A. a large number of similar letters is to be sent
    B. the letters are to be uniform in length and appearance
    C. it is desired to reduce typing errors in correspondence
    D. the office is to carry on a lengthy correspondence with an individual

24._____

25. Of the following, the MOST important factor in determining whether or not an office filing system is effective is that the
    A. information in the files is legible
    B. records in the files are used frequently
    C. information in the files is accurate
    D. records in the files can be located readily

25._____

KEY (CORRECT ANSWERS)

1. B	11. B	21. D
2. D	12. C	22. B
3. C	13. C	23. D
4. B	14. D	24. A
5. A	15. D	25. D
6. D	16. B	
7. A	17. C	
8. D	18. A	
9. C	19. B	
10. D	20. C	

TEST 2

DIRECTIONS: Each question or incomplete statement is followed by several suggested answers or completions. Select the one that BEST answers the question or completes the statement. *PRINT THE LETTER OF THE CORRECT ANSWER IN THE SPACE AT THE RIGHT.*

1. For the office assistant whose duties include frequent recording and transcription of minutes of formal meetings, the one of the following reference works generally considered to be MOST useful is
    A. *Robert's Rules of Order*
    B. *Bartlett's Familiar Quotations*
    C. *World Almanac and Book of Facts*
    D. *Conway's Reference*

    1._____

2. Of the following statements about the numeric system of filing, the one which is CORRECT is that it
    A. is the least accurate of all methods of filing
    B. eliminates the need for cross-referencing
    C. allows for very limited expansion
    D. requires a separate index

    2._____

3. When more than one name or subject is involved in a piece of correspondence to be filed, the office assistant should GENERALLY
    A. prepare a cross-reference sheet
    B. establish a geographical filing system
    C. prepare out-guides
    D. establish a separate index card file for noting such correspondence

    3._____

4. A tickler file is MOST generally used for
    A. identification of material contained in a numeric file
    B. maintenance of a current listing of telephone numbers
    C. follow-up of matters requiring future attention
    D. control of records borrowed or otherwise removed from the files

    4._____

5. In filing, the name Ms. *Ann Catalana-Moss* should GENERALLY be indexed as
    A. Moss, Catalana, Ann (Ms.)
    B. Catalana-Moss, Ann (Ms.)
    C. Ann Catalana-Moss (Ms.)
    D. Moss-Catalana, Ann (Ms.)

    5._____

7

6. An office assistant has a set of four cards, each of which contains one of the following names.
   In alphabetic filing, the FIRST of the cards to be filed is
   A. Ms. Alma John
   B. Mrs. John (Patricia) Edwards
   C. John-Edward School Supplies, Inc.
   D. John H. Edwards

7. Generally, of the following, the name to be filed FIRST in an alphabetical filing system is
   A. Diane Maestro
   B. Diana McElroy
   C. James Mackell
   D. James McKell

8. After checking several times, you are unable to locate a student record in its proper file drawer. The file drawer in question is used constantly by many members of the staff.
   In this situation, the NEXT step you should take in locating the missing record is to
   A. ask another worker to look through the file drawer
   B. determine if there is another copy of the record filed in a different place
   C. find out if the record has been removed by another staff member
   D. wait a day or two and see if the record turns up

9. It is MOST important that an enclosure which is to be mailed with a letter should be put in an envelope so that
   A. any printing on the enclosure will not be visible through the address side of the envelope
   B. it is obvious that there is an enclosure inside the envelope
   C. the enclosure takes up less space than the letter
   D. the person who opens the envelope will pull out both the letter and the enclosure

10. Suppose that one of the student aides with whom you work suggests a change in the filing procedure. He is sure the change will result in increased rates of filing among the other employees.
    The one of the following which you should do FIRST is to
    A. ask him to demonstrate his method in order to determine if he files more quickly than the other employees
    B. ask your supervisor if you may make a change in the filing procedure
    C. ignore the aide's suggestion since he is not a filing expert
    D. tell him to show his method to the other employees and to encourage them to use it

11. It is generally advisable to leave at least six inches of working space in a file drawer. This procedure is MOST useful in
    A. decreasing the number of filing errors
    B. facilitating the sorting of documents and folders
    C. maintaining a regular program of removing inactive records
    D. preventing folders and papers from being torn

11._____

12. Assume that a dictator is briefly interrupted because of a telephone call or other similar matter (no more than three minutes).
    Of the following tasks, the person taking the dictation should NORMALLY use the time to
    A. re-read notes already recorded
    B. tidy the dictator's desk
    C. check the accuracy of the dictator's desk files
    D. return to her own desk to type the dictated material

12._____

13. When typing a preliminary draft of a report, the one of the following which you should generally NOT do is
    A. erase typing errors and deletions rather than cross them out
    B. leave plenty of room at the top, bottom and sides of each page
    C. make only the number of copies that you are asked to make
    D. type double or triple space

13._____

14. The BEST way for a receptionist to deal with a situation in which she must leave her desk for a long time is to
    A. ask someone to take her place while she is away
    B. leave a note or sign on her desk which indicates the time she will return
    C. take a chance that no one will arrive while she is gone and leave her desk unattended
    D. tell a coworker to ask any visitors that arrive to wait until she returns

14._____

15. Suppose that two individuals come up to your desk at the same time. One of them asks you for the location of the nearest public phone. After you answer the question, you turn to the second person who asks you the same question.
    The one of the following actions that would be BEST for you to take in this situation is to
    A. ignore the second person since he obviously overheard your first answer
    B. point out that you just answered the same question and quickly repeat the information
    C. politely repeat the information to the second individual
    D. tell the second person to follow the first to the public telephone

15._____

16. Which of the following names should be filed FIRST in an alphabetical filing system?
    A. Anthony Aarvedsen
    B. William Aaron
    C. Denise Aron
    D. A.J. Arrington

17. New material added to a file folder should USUALLY be inserted
    A. in the order of importance (the most important in front)
    B. in the order of importance (the most important in back)
    C. chronologically (most recent in front)
    D. chronologically (most recent in back)

18. An individual is looking for a name in the White Pages of a telephone directory.
    Which of the following BEST describes the system of filing found there?
    A. alphabetic
    B. sequential
    C. locator
    D. index

19. The MAIN purpose of a tickler file is to
    A. help prevent overlooking matters that require future attention
    B. check on adequacy of past performance
    C. pinpoint responsibility for recurring daily tasks
    D. reduce the volume of material kept in general files

20. Which of the following BEST describes the process of *reconciling* a bank statement?
    A. Analyzing the nature of the expenditures made by the office during the preceding month
    B. Comparing the statement of the bank with the banking records maintained in the office
    C. Determining the liquidity position by reading the bank statement carefully
    D. Checking the service charges noted on the bank statement

21. From the viewpoint of preserving agency or institutional funds, the LEAST acceptable method for making a payment is a check made out to
    A. cash
    B. a company
    C. an individual
    D. a partnership

22. Listed below are four of the steps in the process of preparing correspondence for filing.
    If they were to be put in logical sequence, the SECOND step would be
    A. preparing cross-reference sheets or cards
    B. coding the correspondence using a classification system
    C. sorting the correspondence in the order to be filed
    D. checking for follow-up action required and preparing a follow-up slip

23. The process of *justifying* typed copy involves laying out the copy so that 23._____
    A. each paragraph appears to be approximately the same size
    B. no long words are broken up at the end of a line
    C. the right and left hand margins are even
    D. there is enough room to enter proofreading marks at the end of each line

24. The MOST important reason for a person in charge of a petty cash fund 24._____
    to obtain receipts for payments is that this practice would tend to
    A. decrease robberies by delivery personnel
    B. eliminate the need to keep a record of petty cash expenditures
    C. prove that the fund has been used properly
    D. provide a record of the need for cash in the daily operations of the office

25. You should GENERALLY replenish a petty cash fund 25._____
    A. at regularly established intervals
    B. each time you withdraw a sum
    C. when the amount of cash gets below a certain specified amount
    D. when the fund is completely empty

KEY (CORRECT ANSWERS)

1. A	11. D	21. A
2. D	12. A	22. A
3. A	13. A	23. C
4. C	14. A	24. C
5. B	15. C	25. C
6. D	16. B	
7. C	17. C	
8. C	18. A	
9. D	19. A	
10. A	20. B	

EXAMINATION SECTION
TEST 1

DIRECTIONS: Each question or incomplete statement is followed by several suggested answers or completions. Select the one that BEST answers the question or completes the statement. *PRINT THE LETTER OF THE CORRECT ANSWER IN THE SPACE AT THE RIGHT.*

1. If you open a personal letter by mistake, the one of the following actions which it would generally be BEST for you to take is to

    A. ignore your error, attach the envelope to the letter, and distribute in the usual manner
    B. personally give the addressee the letter without any explanation
    C. place the letter inside the envelope, indicate under your initials that it was opened in error, and give to the addressee
    D. reseal the envelope or place the contents in another envelope and pass on to addressee

2. If you receive a telephone call regarding a matter which your office does not handle, you should FIRST

    A. give the caller the telephone number of the proper office so that he can dial again
    B. offer to transfer the caller to the proper office
    C. suggest that the caller re-dial since he probably dialed incorrectly
    D. tell the caller he has reached the wrong office and then hang up

3. When you answer the telephone, the MOST important reason for identifying yourself and your organization is to

    A. give the caller time to collect his or her thoughts
    B. impress the caller with your courtesy
    C. inform the caller that he or she has reached the right number
    D. set a business-like tone at the beginning of the conversation

4. The one of the following cases in which you would NOT place a special notation in the left margin of a letter that you have typed is when

    A. one of the copies is intended for someone other than the addressee of the letter
    B. you enclose a flyer with the letter
    C. you sign your superior's name to the letter, at his or her request
    D. the letter refers to something being sent under separate cover

5. Suppose that you accidentally cut a letter or enclosure as you are opening an envelope with a paper knife.
   The one of the following that you should do FIRST is to

    A. determine whether the document is important
    B. clip or staple the pieces together and process as usual
    C. mend the cut document with transparent tape
    D. notify the sender that the communication was damaged and request another copy

6. As soon as you pick up the phone, a very angry caller begins immediately to complain about city agencies and *red tape*. He says that he has been shifted to two or three different offices. It turns out that he is seeking information which is not immediately available to you. You believe you know, however, where it can be found.
Which of the following actions is the BEST one for you to take?

   A. To eliminate all confusion, suggest that the caller write the mayor stating explicitly what he wants.
   B. Apologize by telling the caller how busy city agencies now are, but also tell him directly that you do not have the information he needs.
   C. Ask for the caller's telephone number, and assure him you will call back after you have checked further.
   D. Give the caller the name and telephone number of the person who might be able to help, but explain that you are not positive he will get results.

7. Suppose that one of your duties is to dictate responses to routine requests from the public for information. A letter writer asks for information which, as expressed in a one-sentence, explicit agency rule, cannot be given out to the public.
Of the following ways of answering the letter, which is the MOST efficient?

   A. Quote verbatim that section of the agency rules which prohibits giving this information to the public.
   B. Without quoting the rule, explain why you cannot accede to the request and suggest alternative sources.
   C. Describe how carefully the request was considered before classifying it as subject to the rule forbidding the issuance of such information.
   D. Acknowledge receipt of the letter and advise that the requested information is not released to the public.

8. Suppose you assist in supervising a staff which has rather high morale, and your own supervisor asks you to poll the staff to find out who will be able to work overtime this particular evening to help complete emergency work.
Which of the following approaches would be MOST likely to win their cooperation while maintaining their morale?

   A. Tell them that the better assignments will be given only to those who work overtime.
   B. Tell them that occasional overtime is a job requirement.
   C. Assure them they'll be doing you a personal favor.
   D. Let them know clearly why the overtime is needed.

9. Suppose that you have been asked to write and to prepare for reproduction new departmental vacation leave regulations.
After you have written the new regulations, all of which fit on two pages, which one of the following would be the BEST method of reproducing 1,000 copies?

   A. An outside private printer because you can best maintain confidentiality using this technique
   B. Photocopying because the copies will have the best possible appearance
   C. Sending the file to all department employees as printable PDFs
   D. Printing and collating on the office high-volume printer

10. You are in charge of verifying employees' qualifications. This involves telephoning previous employers and schools. One of the applications which you are reviewing contains information which you are almost certain is correct on the basis of what the employee has told you.
    The BEST thing to do is to

    A. check the information again with the employer
    B. perform the required verification procedures
    C. accept the information as valid
    D. ask a superior to verify the information

11. The practice of immediately identifying oneself and one's place of employment when contacting persons on the telephone is

    A. *good* because the receiver of the call can quickly identify the caller and establish a frame of reference
    B. *good* because it helps to set the caller at ease with the other party
    C. *poor* because it is not necessary to divulge that information when making general calls
    D. *poor* because it takes longer to arrive at the topic to be discussed

12. Which one of the following should be the MOST important overall consideration when preparing a recommendation to automate a large-scale office activity?
    The

    A. number of models of automated equipment available
    B. benefits and costs of automation
    C. fears and resistance of affected employees
    D. experience of offices which have automated similar activities

13. A tickler file is MOST appropriate for filing materials

    A. chronologically according to date they were received
    B. alphabetically by name
    C. alphabetically by subject
    D. chronologically according to date they should be followed up

14. Which of the following is the BEST reason for decentralizing rather then centralizing the use of duplicating machines?

    A. Developing and retaining efficient duplicating machine operators
    B. Facilitating supervision of duplicating services
    C. Motivating employees to produce legible duplicated copies
    D. Placing the duplicating machines where they are most convenient and most frequently used

15. Window envelopes are sometimes considered preferable to individually addressed envelopes PRIMARILY because

    A. window envelopes are available in standard sizes for all purposes
    B. window envelopes are more attractive and official-looking
    C. the use of window envelopes eliminates the risk of inserting a letter in the wrong envelope
    D. the use of window envelopes requires neater typing

16. In planning the layout of a new office, the utilization of space and the arrangement of staff, furnishings, and equipment should usually be MOST influenced by the

    A. gross square footage
    B. status differences in the chain of command
    C. framework of informal relationships among employees
    D. activities to be performed

17. Office forms sometimes consist of several copies, each of a different color. The MAIN reason for using different colors is to

    A. make a favorable impression on the users of the form
    B. distinguish each copy from the others
    C. facilitate the preparation of legible carbon copies
    D. reduce cost, since using colored stock permits recycling of paper

18. Which of the following is the BEST justification for obtaining a photocopying machine for the office?

    A. A photocopying machine can produce an unlimited number of copies at a low fixed cost per copy.
    B. Employees need little training in operating a photocopying machine.
    C. Office costs will be reduced and efficiency increased.
    D. The legibility of a photocopy generally is superior to copy produced by any other office duplicating device.

19. An administrative officer in charge of a small fund for buying office supplies has just written a check to Charles Laird, a supplier, and has sent the check by messenger to him. A half-hour later, the messenger telephones the administrative officer. He has lost the check.
    Which of the following is the MOST important action for the administrative officer to take under these circumstances?

    A. Ask the messenger to return and write a report describing the loss of the check.
    B. Make a note on the performance record of the messenger who lost the check.
    C. Take the necessary steps to have payment stopped on the check.
    D. Refrain from doing anything since the check may be found shortly.

20. A petty cash fund is set up PRIMARILY to

    A. take care of small investments that must be made from time to time
    B. take care of small expenses that arise from time to time
    C. provide a fund to be used as the office wants to use it with little need to maintain records
    D. take care of expenses that develop during emergencies such as machine breakdowns and fires

21. Your superior has asked you to send a package from your agency to a government agency in another city. He has written out the message and has indicated the name of the government agency.
    When you prepare the package for mailing, which of the following items that your superior has not mentioned must you be sure to include?

A. Today's date
B. The full address of the government agency
C. A polite opening such as *Dear Sirs*
D. A final sentence such as *We would appreciate hearing from your agency in reply as soon as is convenient for you*

22. In addition to the original piece of correspondence, one should USUALLY also have typed

    A. a single copy
    B. as many copies as can be typed at one time
    C. no more copies than are needed
    D. two copies

23. The one of the following which is the BEST procedure to follow when making a short insert in a completed dictation is to

    A. label the insert with a letter and indicate the position of the insert in the text by writing the identifying letter in the proper place
    B. squeeze the insert into its proper place within the main text of the dictation
    C. take down the insert and check the placement with the person who dictated when you are ready to transcribe your notes
    D. transcribe the dictation into longhand, including the insert in its proper position

24. The one of the following procedures which will be MOST efficient in helping you to quickly open your dictation notebook to a clean sheet is to

    A. clip or place a rubberband around the used portion of the notebook
    B. leave the book out and open to a clean page when not in use
    C. transcribe each dictation after it is given and rip out the used pages
    D. use a book marker to indicate which portion of the notebook has been used

25. The purpose of dating your dictation notebooks is GENERALLY to

    A. enable you to easily refer to your notes at a later date
    B. ensure that you transcribe your notes in the order in which they were dictated
    C. set up a precise record-keeping procedure
    D. show your employer that you pay attention to detail

KEY (CORRECT ANSWERS)

1. C
2. B
3. C
4. C
5. C

6. C
7. A
8. D
9. D
10. B

11. A
12. B
13. D
14. D
15. C

16. D
17. B
18. C
19. C
20. B

21. B
22. C
23. A
24. A
25. A

TEST 2

DIRECTIONS: Each question or incomplete statement is followed by several suggested answers or completions. Select the one that BEST answers the question or completes the statement. *PRINT THE LETTER OF THE CORRECT ANSWER IN THE SPACE AT THE RIGHT.*

1. With regard to typed correspondence received by most offices, which of the following is the GREATEST problem?   1.____

    A. Verbosity
    B. Illegibility
    C. Improper folding
    D. Excessive copies

2. Of the following, the GREATEST advantage of flash drives over rewritable CD storage is that they   2.____

    A. are portable
    B. are both smaller and lighter
    C. contain more storage space
    D. allow files to be deleted to free space

3. Suppose that a large quantity of information is in the files which are located a good distance from your desk. Almost every worker in your office must use these files constantly. Your duties in particular require that you daily refer to about 25 of the same items. They are short, one-page items distributed throughout the files. In this situation, your BEST course would be to   3.____

    A. take the items that you use daily from the files and keep them on your desk, inserting *out cards* in their place
    B. go to the files each time you need the information so that the items will be there when other workers need them
    C. make xerox copies of the information you use most frequently and keep them in your desk for ready reference
    D. label the items you use most often with different colored tabs for immediate identification

4. Of the following, the MOST important advantage of preparing manuals of office procedures in loose-leaf form is that this form   4.____

    A. permits several employees to use different sections simultaneously
    B. facilitates the addition of new material and the removal of obsolete material
    C. is more readily arranged in alphabetical order
    D. reduces the need for cross-references to locate material carried under several headings

5. Suppose that you establish a new clerical procedure for the unit you supervise. Your keeping a close check on the time required by your staff to handle the new procedure is WISE mainly because such a check will find out   5.____

    A. whether your subordinates know how to handle the new procedure
    B. whether a revision of the unit's work schedule will be necessary as a result of the new procedure
    C. what attitude your employees have toward the new procedure
    D. what alterations in job descriptions will be necessitated by the new procedure

6. The numbered statements below relate to the stenographic skill of taking dictation. According to authorities on secretarial practices, which of these are generally recommended guides to development of efficient stenographic skills?

STATEMENTS
1. A stenographer should date her notebook daily to facilitate locating certain notes at a later time.
2. A stenographer should make corrections of grammatical mistakes while her boss is dictating to her.
3. A stenographer should draw a line through the dictated matter in her notebook after she has transcribed it.
4. A stenographer should write in longhand unfamiliar names and addresses dictated to her.

The CORRECT answer is:

A. Only Statements 1, 2, and 3 are generally recommended guides.
B. Only Statements 2, 3, and 4 are generally recommended guides.
C. Only Statements 1, 3, and 4 are generally recommended guides.
D. All four statements are generally recommended guides.

7. According to generally recognized rules of filing in an alphabetic filing system, the one of the following names which normally should be filed LAST is

A. Department of Education, New York State
B. F.B.I.
C. Police Department of New York City
D. P.S. 81 of New York City

8. Which one of the following forms for the typed name of the dictator in the closing lines of a letter is generally MOST acceptable in the United States?

A. (Dr.) James F. Fenton
B. Dr. James F. Fenton
C. Mr. James F. Fenton, Ph.D.
D. James F. Fenton

9. Which of the following is, MOST generally, a rule to be followed when typing a rough draft?

A. The copy should be single spaced.
B. The copy should be triple spaced.
C. There is no need for including footnotes.
D. Errors must be neatly corrected.

10. An office assistant needs a synonym.
Of the following, the book which she would find MOST useful is

A. a world atlas
B. BARTLETT'S FAMILIAR QUOTATIONS
C. a manual of style
D. a thesaurus

11. Of the following examples of footnotes, the one that is expressed in the MOST generally accepted standard form is:

    A. Johnson, T.F. (Dr.), <u>English for Everyone</u>, 3rd or 4th edition; New York City Linton Publishing Company, p. 467
    B. Frank Taylor, <u>English for Today</u> (New York: Rayton Publishing Company, 1971), p. 156
    C. Ralph Wilden, <u>English for Tomorrow,</u> Reynolds Publishing Company, England, p. 451
    D. Quinn, David, Yesterday's English (New York: Baldwin Publishing Company, 1972), p. 431

12. Standard procedures are used in offices PRIMARILY because

    A. an office is a happier place if everyone is doing the tasks in the same manner
    B. particular ways of doing jobs are considered more efficient than other ways
    C. it is good discipline for workers to follow standard procedures approved by the supervisor
    D. supervisors generally don't want workers to be creative in planning their work

13. Assume that an office assistant has the responsibility for compiling, typing, and mailing a preliminary announcement of Spring term course offerings. The announcement will go to approximately 900 currently enrolled students. Assuming that the following equipment is available for use, the MOST EFFECTIVE method for distributing the announcement to all 900 students is to

    A. e-mail it as a text document using the electronic student mailing list
    B. post the announcement as a PDF document for download on the department website
    C. send it by fax
    D. post the announcement and leave copies in buildings around campus

14. *Justified typing* is a term that refers MOST specifically to typewriting copy

    A. that has been edited and for which final copy is being prepared
    B. in a form that allows for an even right-hand margin
    C. with a predetermined vertical placement for each alternate line
    D. that has been approved by the supervisor and his superior

15. Which one of the following is the BEST form for the address in a letter?

    A. Mr. John Jones
       Vice President, The Universal Printing Company
       1220 Fifth Avenue
       New York, 10023 New York
    B. Mr. John Jones, Vice President
       The Universal Printing Company
       1220 Fifth Avenue
       New York, New York 10023
    C. Mr. John Jones, Vice President, The Universal Printing Company
       1220 Fifth Avenue
       New York, New York 10023

D. Mr. John Jones Vice President,
   The Universal Printing Company
   1220 Fifth Avenue
   New York, 10023 New York

16. Of the following, the CHIEF advantage of the use of window envelopes over ordinary envelopes is that window envelopes

    A. eliminate the need for addressing envelopes
    B. protect the confidential nature of enclosed material
    C. cost less to buy than ordinary envelopes
    D. reduce the danger of the address becoming illegible

17. In the complimentary close of a business letter, the FIRST letter of _____ should be capitalized.

    A. all the words
    B. none of the words
    C. only the first word
    D. only the last word

18. Assume that one of your duties is to procure needed office supplies from the supply room. You are permitted to draw supplies every two weeks.
    The one of the following which would be the MOST desirable practice for you to follow in obtaining supplies is to

    A. obtain a quantity of supplies sufficient to last for several months to make certain that enough supplies are always on hand
    B. determine the minimum supply necessary to keep on hand for the various items and obtain an additional quantity as soon as possible after the supply on hand has been reduced to this minimum
    C. review the supplies once a month to determine what items have been exhausted and obtain an additional quantity as soon as possible
    D. obtain a supply of an item as soon after it has been exhausted as is possible

19. Some offices that keep carbon copies of letters use several different colors of carbon paper for making carbon copies.
    Of the following, the CHIEF reason for using different colors of carbon paper is to

    A. facilitate identification of different types of letters in the files
    B. relieve the monotony of typing and filing carbon copies
    C. reduce the costs of preparing carbon copies
    D. utilize both sides of the carbon paper for typing

20. Your supervisor asks you to post an online ad for freelance designers interested in submitting samples for a new company logo. Prospective workers should be proficient in which of the following software?

    A. Microsoft Word
    B. Adobe Acrobat Pro
    C. Adobe Illustrator
    D. Microsoft PowerPoint

21. Gary Thompson is applying for a position with the firm of Gray and Williams.
    Which letter should be filed in top position in the *Application* folder?

    A. A letter of recommendation written on September 18 by Johnson & Smith
    B. Williams' letter of October 8 requesting further details regarding Thompson's experience

C. Thompson's letter of September 8 making application for a position as sales manager
D. Letter of September 20 from Alfred Jackson recommending Thompson for the job

22. The USUAL arrangement in indexing the names of the First National Bank, Toledo, is

 A. First National Bank, Toledo, Ohio
 B. Ohio, First National Bank, Toledo
 C. Toledo, First National Bank, Ohio
 D. Ohio, Toledo, First National Bank

23. A single line through typed text indicating that it's incorrect or invalid is known as a(n)

 A. underline
 B. strikethrough
 C. line font
 D. eraser

24. A typical e-mail with an attachment should contain all of the following for successful transmittal EXCEPT

 A. recipient's address
 B. file attachment
 C. body text
 D. description of attachment

25. The subject line in a letter is USUALLY typed a _____ space below the _____.

 A. single; inside address
 B. single; salutation
 C. double; inside address
 D. double; salutation

KEY (CORRECT ANSWERS)

1.	A	11.	B
2.	C	12.	B
3.	C	13.	A
4.	B	14.	B
5.	B	15.	B
6.	C	16.	A
7.	D	17.	C
8.	D	18.	B
9.	B	19.	A
10.	D	20.	C

21. B
22. A
23. B
24. D
25. D

EXAMINATION SECTION

TEST 1

PART A. VOCABULARY

Questions 1-20.

DIRECTIONS: In each of the following groups of words, one word or phrase means the same as the word given. Indicate the related word or phrase by choosing the corresponding letter. PRINT THE LETTER OF THE CORRECT ANSWER IN THE SPACE AT THE RIGHT.

1. impious
   - A. irreverent
   - B. friendly
   - C. hostile
   - D. mischievous

   1._____

2. bode
   - A. travel
   - B. appease
   - C. dismay
   - D. portend

   2._____

3. martinet
   - A. attorney
   - B. physician
   - C. disciplinarian
   - D. performer

   3._____

4. obtuse
   - A. solid
   - B. spiteful
   - C. cheerful
   - D. stupid

   4._____

5. comely
   - A. pretty
   - B. common
   - C. congruent
   - D. perfidious

   5._____

6. obfuscate
   - A. obscure
   - B. remove
   - C. clarify
   - D. decline

   6._____

7. diurnal
   - A. weekly
   - B. daily
   - C. monthly
   - D. yearly

   7._____

8. upbraid
   - A. scold
   - B. commend
   - C. congratulate
   - D. repair

   8._____

9. veracious
   - A. fretful
   - B. truthful
   - C. hungry
   - D. distasteful

   9._____

10. feckless
    - A. uncertain
    - B. irresponsible
    - C. insecure
    - D. timid

    10._____

11. vainglorious
    A. frustrated   B. exuberant
    C. boastful   D. petulant

    11._____

12. mendacity
    A. unknown   B. untruth
    C. uncertain   D. unkind

    12._____

13. respite
    A. postponement   B. decline
    C. pundit   D. resuscitator

    13._____

14. intrepid
    A. cowardly   B. weakly
    C. disdainful   D. fearless

    14._____

15. fortuitously
    A. thoroughly   B. consciously
    C. accidentally   D. luckily

    15._____

16. dastardly
    A. pernicious   B. haughty
    C. cowardly   D. elegiacal

    16._____

17. salubrious
    A. brilliant   B. healthful
    C. flowering   D. amusing

    17._____

18. assuage
    A. pacify   B. confuse
    C. worsen   D. distort

    18._____

19. fatuous
    A. unreal   B. fattish
    C. slim   D. silly

    19._____

20. tractable
    A. uncontrollable   B. eager
    C. dubious   D. docile

    20._____

Questions 21-40.

DIRECTIONS: In each of the following groups of words, one word or phrase means most nearly the opposite of the word on the left. Indicate the related word or phrase by choosing the corresponding letter. PRINT THE LETTER OF THE CORRECT ANSWER IN THE SPACE AT THE RIGHT.

21. timorous
    A. timid   B. tardy
    C. punctual   D. bold

    21._____

22. debilitate
    A. harass
    B. annoy
    C. strengthen
    D. affix

    22._____

23. mutable
    A. changeable
    B. lovable
    C. constant
    D. spiteful

    23._____

24. deprecate
    A. plead for
    B. dishonor
    C. contrive
    D. aver

    24._____

25. secular
    A. musical
    B. worldly
    C. sacred
    D. hospitable

    25._____

26. vitiate
    A. remove
    B. spoil
    C. lower
    D. purify

    26._____

27. recondite
    A. confused
    B. hidden
    C. clear
    D. unpaid

    27._____

28. parsimonious
    A. frugal
    B. obdurate
    C. officious
    D. extravagant

    28._____

29. nascent
    A. terminating
    B. commencing
    C. erecting
    D. halting

    29._____

30. culpable
    A. blameless
    B. childless
    C. courteous
    D. trustworthy

    30._____

31. nepotism
    A. favoritism
    B. indifference
    C. impartiality
    D. apathy

    31._____

32. surfeit
    A. plentiful
    B. insufficient
    C. distasteful
    D. affected

    32._____

33. odious
    A. hateful
    B. sinful
    C. inoffensive
    D. spiteful

    33._____

34. inveterate
    A. habitual
    B. experienced
    C. dauntless
    D. inexperienced

    34._____

35. indolent
    A. industrious
    B. lazy
    C. opulent
    D. corpulent

36. venial
    A. sacrificial
    B. unrealistic
    C. unpardonable
    D. sanguine

37. rubicund
    A. ruddy
    B. pale
    C. rotund
    D. roseate

38. espouse
    A. support
    B. relate
    C. sue
    D. oppose

39. lugubrious
    A. doleful
    B. mournful
    C. happy
    D. malicious

40. emend
    A. improve
    B. worsen
    C. correct
    D. ignore

PART B. SPELLING

Questions 41-60.

DIRECTIONS: In each of the following groups of words, one word is misspelled. Indicate the misspelled word by choosing the corresponding letter. PRINT THE LETTER OF THE CORRECT ANSWER IN THE SPACE AT THE RIGHT.

41. A. annotation
    B. per cent
    C. inoculate
    D. indispensible

42. A. flammable
    B. impresario
    C. accredited
    D. guerrilla

43. A. desiccate
    B. boundry
    C. anoint
    D. mattress

44. A. acquitted
    B. adolescence
    C. heavyness
    D. irascible

45. A. ukulele
    B. presumptious
    C. isosceles
    D. Pittsburgh

46. A. innate
    B. cannoneer
    C. passtime
    D. auditorium

47.	A. hinderance B. benefited C. embarrass D. syllabus	47._____
48.	A. Cincinnati B. pavilion C. ebulient D. questionnaire	48._____
49.	A. dilletante B. liquefy C. physiology D. proscribe	49._____
50.	A. harass B. vilify C. similar D. supercede	50._____
51.	A. connoisseur B. ancillary C. coliseum D. buccaneer	51._____
52.	A. auxiliary B. plebescite C. millionaire D. Philippines	52._____
53.	A. educable B. beneficent C. medalion D. corollary	53._____
54.	A. miscellaneous B. vicissitude C. imbroglio D. temperment	54._____
55.	A. familiar B. millennium C. privilege D. notable	55._____
56.	A. chagrined B. demurred C. holacoust D. underrate	56._____
57.	A. occured B. accede C. annulling D. parallel	57._____
58.	A. cotillion B. Albuquerque C. inveigle D. rememberance	58._____
59.	A. chrysanthemum B. sexogenarian C. drily D. enameled	59._____
60.	A. prerogative B. extracurricular C. irridescent D. rarefy	60._____

PART C. GRAMMAR, USAGE, SENTENCE STRUCTURE, DICTION, CAPITALIZATION, AND PUNCTUATION

Questions 61-80.

DIRECTIONS: In each of the following groups of sentences, one sentence is incorrect because it includes an error in grammar, usage, sentence structure, diction, capitalization, or punctuation. Indicate the incorrect sentence by choosing the corresponding letter. PRINT THE LETTER OF THE CORRECT ANSWER IN THE SPACE AT THE RIGHT.

61.
- A. We shall have to leave it to the jury to make a determination of the facts.
- B. His precision resulted in a nice discrimination between their relative merits.
- C. Green vegetables are healthy foods.
- D. We shall attempt to ascertain whether there has been any tampering with the lock.

62.
- A. Have you made any definitive plans which may be applied to budget preparation?
- B. We planned on taking a walking trip through the mountains.
- C. I would much rather he had called me after we had taken the trip.
- D. Do you believe that he has a predisposition toward that kind of response?

63.
- A. He carried out the orders with great dispatch but with little effect.
- B. The cook's overbearing manner overawed his employer.
- C. All of us shall partake of the benefits of exercise.
- D. Miss Smith made less errors than the other typists.

64.
- A. I believe that we are liable to have good weather tomorrow.
- B. From what I could see, I though he acted like the others.
- C. Perpetual motion is an idea which is not unthinkable.
- D. Many of us taxpayers are displeased with the service.

65.
- A. She was incredulous when I told her the incredible tale.
- B. She was told that the symptoms would disappear within a week.
- C. If possible, I should like to sit in front of the very tall couple.
- D. Punish whomever disobeys our commands.

66.
- A. The men were trapped inside the cave for four days.
- B. The man seated in back of me was talking throughout the play.
- C. He told me that he doesn't know whether he will be able to visit us.
- D. Please bring me the pair of scissors from the table.

67.
  A. He was charged with having committed many larcenous acts.
  B. Material wealth is certainly not something to be dismissed cavalierly.
  C. He is one of those people who do everything promptly.
  D. I hope to be able to retaliate for the assistance you have given me.

68.
  A. Have you noted the unusual phenomena to be seen in that portion of the heavens?
  B. The data is as accurate as it is possible to make it.
  C. The enormity of the crime was such that we could not comprehend it.
  D. The collection of monies from some clients was long overdue.

69.
  A. What you are doing is not really different than what I had suggested.
  B. The enormousness of the animal was enough to make her gasp.
  C. The judge brought in a decision which aroused antagonism in the community.
  D. I asked the monitor to take the papers to the principal.

70.
  A. He talks as if he were tired.
  B. He amended his declaration to include additional income.
  C. I know that he would have succeeded if he had tried.
  D. Whom does Mrs. Jones think wrote the play?

71.
  A. The stone made a very angry bruise on his forearm.
  B. He said to me: "I'm very mad at you."
  C. In all likelihood, we shall be unable to go to the fair.
  D. He would have liked to go to the theatre with us.

72.
  A. The lawyers tried to settle the case out of court.
  B. "Get out of my life!" she cried.
  C. Walking down the road, the lake comes into view.
  D. The loan which I received from the bank helped me to keep the business going.

73.
  A. I shall go with you providing that we return home early.
  B. He has been providing us with excellent baked goods for many years.
  C. It has been proved, to my satisfaction, to be correct.
  D. Whether we go or not is for you to decide.

8 (#1)

74.
- A. He does not seem able to present a logical and convincing argument.
- B. Each of the goaltenders was trying to protect his respective cage.
- C. He said, "I shall go there directly."
- D. The reason he was late was on account of the delay in transportation.

74._____

75.
- A. Her mien revealed her abhorrence of his actions.
- B. She used a great deal of rope so it would not come apart.
- C. After he had lived among them, he found much to admire in their way of life.
- D. He waited patiently for the fish to snatch at the bait.

75._____

76.
- A. As a result of constant exposure to the elements, he took sick and required medical attention.
- B. Although the automobile is very old, we think it can still be used for a long trip.
- C. He purchased all the supplies she requested with one exception.
- D. He has repeated the story so frequently that I think he has begun to believe it.

76._____

77.
- A. It is the noise made by the crickets that you hear.
- B. She told us that she would be at home on Sunday.
- C. She said, "If I'm not there on time, don't wait on me."
- D. Please try to maintain a cheerful disposition under any and all provocations.

77._____

78.
- A. Who is the tallest boy in the class?
- B. Where shall I look to find a similar kind of stone?
- C. The horse took the jumps with a great deal of ease.
- D. He is as good, if not better than, any other jumper in the country.

78._____

79.
- A. Which of the two machines would be the most practical?
- B. All of us are entitled to a reply if we are to determine whether you should remain as a member of the club.
- C. Everyone who was listening got to his feet and applauded.
- D. There was no indication from his actions that he knew he was wrong.

79._____

80.
- A. I beg leave to call upon you in case of an emergency.
- B. Do not deter me from carrying out the demands of my office.
- C. Please see me irregardless of the time of day.
- D. The intrepid captain shouted: "Into the fray!"

80._____

PART D. RELATED INFORMATION

Questions 81-100.

DIRECTIONS: In each of the following questions, there are three incorrect answers and one correct answer. Indicate the correct answer by choosing the corresponding letter. PRINT THE LETTER OF THE CORRECT ANSWER IN THE SPACE AT THE RIGHT.

81. A collection of maps and statistical information in regard to population may be found in the
    A. Roget's Thesaurus
    B. U. S. Government Printing Office Style Manual
    C. Thomas' Register of American Manufacturers
    D. Atlas

81._____

82. A letter which usually accompanies a formal report is referred to as a(n)
    A. accompanying letter   B. explanatory letter
    C. informational letter   D. transmittal letter

82._____

83. The official records of meetings or conferences are referred to as the
    A. notes   B. transcripts
    C. minutes   D. data

83._____

84. Increases or decreases over a period of time can be represented most effectively by the use of a
    A. bar graph   B. line graph
    C. circle graph   D. Pictograph

84._____

85. A secretary should "proof" her typewritten material
    A. by using the computer's spell-check function
    B. line by line while she is typing the material
    C. after it has been removed from the printer and photocopied
    D. after it has been completed and again after it is removed from the printer

85._____

86. "Swingline" is the trade name of a
    A. perforator   B. jogger
    C. stapler   D. collator

86._____

87. The weight of correspondence paper most widely used in business offices is
    A. 9 pounds   B. 13 pounds
    C. 16 pounds   D. 20 pounds

87._____

88. The schedule of business to be considered and discussed at a conference is referred to as the
    A. agenda   B. itinerary
    C. addenda   D. proceedings

88._____

89. Helvetica is an example of
    A. serif font
    B. sans serif font
    C. a drop cap
    D. a header style

89._____

90. Concise biographical data and the addresses of important living men and women of the United States may be found in
    A. "Who's Who in America"
    B. "The World Almanac"
    C. "Information Please Almanac"
    D. "Mac Rae's Blue Book"

90._____

91. The correct abbreviation for "in the same place" is
    A. ibid.
    B. id.
    C. i.e.
    D. e.g.

91._____

92. The practice of issuing bills to customers at regularly stated intervals during the course of a month is referred to as
    A. planned billing
    B. differentiated billing
    C. cycle billing
    D. systematic billing

92._____

93. To create a spreadsheet, a secretary would use
    A. Microsoft Word
    B. Microsoft Excel
    C. Microsoft PowerPoint
    D. Adobe Acrobat

93._____

94. Roget's Thesaurus is most similar to a book of
    A. antonyms
    B. homonyms
    C. synonyms
    D. proverbs

94._____

95. The salutation and the complimentary close are eliminated in the
    A. semi-block style letter
    B. indented style letter
    C. simplified format letter
    D. block style letter

95._____

96. The word which is incorrectly syllabicated is
    A. prod uct
    B. knowl edge
    C. ship ped
    D. scheme

96._____

97. The most effective visual aid for depicting the percentages of a whole is a
    A. bar graph
    B. line graph
    C. flow chart
    D. pie chart

97._____

98. An indorsement which includes only the signature of the payee is known as a
    A. blank indorsement
    B. qualified indorsement
    C. restrictive indorsement
    D. special indorsement

98._____

99. The best font size (in points) for typing a business letter is
    A. 8
    B. 12
    C. 14
    D. 18

99._____

100. The reference book which is used most frequently by secretaries is the   100._____
    A. almanac   B. gazetteer
    C. book of quotations   D. dictionary

PART E. FILING

Questions 101-105.

DIRECTIONS: In each of the following questions on filing, three groups of names are arranged correctly and one group is arranged incorrectly. Indicate the group that is arranged incorrectly by choosing the corresponding letter. PRINT THE LETTER OF THE CORRECT ANSWER IN THE SPACE AT THE RIGHT.

101.   101._____
    A. Emory & Sons; Emory, Steuart; Emory, Stewart; Emory, T. E.
    B. Erdlund, Edward; Erdlunda, Mary; Erdlunds, Arnold; Erdlundton, Albert
    C. Allan-Jones, Sylvia; The Allan-Jones Tire Corp.; Allan, Robert; Allan, Roberta
    D. Frank, Peter; Frank & Peters; Franks, George; Franks, George N.

102.   102._____
    A. Harris, Harriet; Harris, Harriette; Harriss, Harold; Harriss, Hyman
    B. St. George, Vivian; St. George, Vivyan; St. George, Vivyenne; Saint, George W.
    C. Gorman, Esmond; Gorman, Esmonda; Gorman, Lila; O'Gorman, Linda
    D. German, Norbert; Germans, Norbert; Germansky, Nilda; Germansky, Norman

103.   103._____
    A. Murtagh, Muriel; Murtagh, Norton; Murtagh & Nortons; Murtagh & Sons
    B. Nestor, G. C.; Nestor & George; Nestor, George C.; Nestoris, Alan
    C. Hinton, Leslie; Hinton, Lester; Hinton, Lester A.; Hinton Linda
    D. Hilton, Harry; Hilton, A. Harry; Hilton, Harry G.; Hiltons, Mary

104.   104._____
    A. Church, George; Church, Georgine; Church & Gibbons; Churchly, Bette
    B. Edwards, A. Maxwell; Edwards, Martin A.; Edwardes, Peter; Edwards, S.
    C. Danton, Daniel; Danton & Edwards; The Danton Shoe Co.; D'Antun, P.
    D. Darcy, Thomas; Darcy, Walter; D'Arcy, William; Darcy, Worth A.

12 (#1)

105.
- A. Oster, Vernon; Oster & Weed; Ostera, Nancy; Ostera, P. T.
- B. Peter, Lyman; Perter, Nelson; Peters, William; Peters, William T.
- C. Wilson, Martin; Wilson and Morton; Wilson Weaving Co.; Wilson, Wilbert
- D. Wood, Charles; Woods, Chalmers; Woods, Melvin; Woods, Melvin C.

105._____

PART F. NUMBER RELATIONSHIP

Questions 106-110.

DIRECTIONS: Each series of numbers is made up according to a certain rule or order. Indicate the <u>next</u> <u>number</u> in the series by choosing the corresponding letter. PRINT THE LETTER OF THE CORRECT ANSWER IN THE SPACE AT THE RIGHT.

106. 7, 21, 42, 126, 252, _____
 A. 275 B. 294
 C. 378 D. 756

106._____

107. 4, 10, 7, 13, 10, 16, _____
 A. 13 B. 12
 C. 14 D. 18

107._____

108. 9, 27, 25, 75, 73, 219, _____
 A. 217 B. 216
 C. 222 D. 637

108._____

109. 3, 9, 10, 30, 31, 93, _____
 A. 91 B. 92
 C. 94 D. 83

109._____

110. 12, 6, 24, 12, 48, 24, _____
 A. 72 B. 96
 C. 144 D. none of the above

110._____

PART G. READING COMPREHENSION

DIRECTIONS: Each of the following passages is followed by three numbered multiple-choice questions. Read the passage and then indicate the correct answer relating to it by choosing the corresponding letter. PRINT THE LETTER OF THE CORRECT ANSWER IN THE SPACE AT THE RIGHT.

Questions 111-113.

The achievement of good human relations is essential if a business office is to produce at top efficiency and is to be a pleasant place in which to work. All office workers play an important role in handling problems in human relations. They should, therefore, strive to acquire the understanding, tactfulness, and awareness necessary to deal effectively with actual office situations involving co-workers on all levels. Only in this way can they truly become responsible, interested, cooperative, and helpful members of the staff.

111. The selection implies that the most important value of good human relations in an office is to develop
 A. efficiency
 B. cooperativeness
 C. tact
 D. pleasantness and efficiency

111._____

112. Office workers should acquire understanding in dealing with
 A. co-workers
 B. subordinates
 C. superiors
 D. all members of the staff

112._____

113. The selection indicates that a highly competent secretary who is also very argumentative is meeting office requirements
 A. wholly
 B. partly
 C. slightly
 D. not at all

113._____

Questions 114-116.

In dealing with visitors to the school office, the school secretary must use initiative, tact, and good judgment. All visitors should be greeted promptly and courteously. The nature of their business should be determined quickly and handled expeditiously. Frequently, the secretary should be able to handle requests, receipts, deliveries, or passes herself. Her judgment should determine when a visitor should see members of the staff or the principal. Serious problems or doubtful cases should be referred to a supervisor.

114. In general, visitors should be handled by the
 A. school secretary
 B. principal
 C. appropriate supervisor
 D. person who is free

114._____

115. It is wide to obtain the following information from visitors
 A. name
 B. nature of business
 C. address
 D. problems they have

115._____

116. All visitors who wish to see members of the staff should   116._____
    A. be permitted to do so
    B. produce identification
    C. do so for valid reasons only
    D. be processed by a supervisor

Questions 117-119.

Information regarding payroll status, salary differentials, promotional salary increments, deductions, and pension payments should be given to all members of the staff who have questions regarding these items. On occasion, if the secretary is uncertain regarding the information, the staff member should be referred to the principal or the appropriate agency. No question by a staff member regarding payroll status should be brushed aside as immaterial or irrelevant. The school secretary must always try to handle the question or pass it on to the person who can handle it.

117. If a teacher is dissatisfied with information regarding her salary status, as   117._____
    given by the school secretary, the matter should be
    A. dropped
    B. passed on to the principal
    C. passed on by the secretary to proper agency or the principal
    D. made a basis for grievance procedures

118. The following is an adequate summary of the above paragraph   118._____
    A. the secretary must handle all payroll matters
    B. the secretary must handle all payroll matters or know who can handle them
    C. the secretary or the principal must handle all payroll matters
    D. payroll matters too difficult to handle must be followed up until they are solved

119. The selection implies that   119._____
    A. many teachers ask immaterial questions regarding payroll status
    B. few teachers ask irrelevant pension questions
    C. no teachers ask immaterial salary questions
    D. no question regarding salary should be considered irrelevant

Questions 120-122.

The necessity for good speech on the part of the school secretary cannot be overstated. The school secretary must deal with the general public, the pupils, the members of the staff, and the school supervisors. In every situation which involves the general public, the secretary serves as a representative of the school. In dealing with pupils, the secretary's speech must serve as a model from which students may guide themselves. Slang, colloquialisms, malapropisms, and local dialects must be avoided.

120. The selection implies that the speech pattern of the secretary must be   120._____
    A. perfect   B. very good
    C. average   D. on a level with that of the pupils

121. The last sentence indicates that slang
    A. is acceptable
    B. occurs in all speech
    C. might be used occasionally
    D. should be shunned

121._____

122. The selection implies that the speech of pupils
    A. may be influenced
    B. does not change readily
    C. is generally good
    D. is generally poor

122._____

Questions 123-125.

The school secretary who is engaged in the task of filing records and correspondence should follow a general set of rules. Items which are filed should be available to other secretaries or to supervisors quickly and easily by means of the application of a modicum of common sense and good judgment. Items which, by their nature, may be difficult to find should be cross-indexed. Folders and drawers should be neatly and accurately labeled. There should never be a large accumulation of papers which have not bee filed.

123. A good general rule to follow in filing is that materials should be
    A. placed in folders quickly
    B. neatly stored
    C. readily available
    D. cross-indexed

123._____

124. Items that are filed should be available to
    A. the secretary charged with the task of filing
    B. secretaries and supervisors
    C. school personnel
    D. the principal

124._____

125. A modicum of common sense means
    A. an average amount of common sense
    B. a great deal of common sense
    C. a little common sense
    D. no common sense

125._____

16 (#1)

PART H. ARITHMETIC

Questions 126-15.

DIRECTIONS: In each of the following problems, there are three incorrect answers and one correct answer. Indicate the correct answer by choosing the corresponding letter. PRINT THE LETTER OF THE CORRECT ANSWER IN THE SPACE AT THE RIGHT.

126. Donald Smith earns $8.60 an hour for forty hours a week, with time and a half for all hours over forty. Last week his total earnings amounted to $421.40. He worked
   A. 46 hours   B. 47 hours
   C. 48 hours   D. 49 hours

126._____

127. Mr. Jones desires to sell an article costing $28 at a gross profit of 30% of the selling price, and to allow a trade discount of 20% of the list price. The list price of the article should be
   A. $43.68   B. $45.50
   C. $48.00   D. $50.00

127._____

128. The gauge of an oil storage tank in an elementary school indicates 1/5 full. After a truck delivers 945 gallons of oil, the gauge indicates 4/5 full. The capacity of the tank is
   A. 1260 gallons   B. 1575 gallons
   C. 1625 gallons   D. 1890 gallons

128._____

129. An invoice dated April 3, terms 3/10, 2/30, net/60, was paid in full with a check for $787.92 on May 1. The amount of the invoice was
   A. $772.16   B. $787.92
   C. $804.00   D. $812.29

129._____

130. Two pipes supply the water for the swimming pool at Bixby High School. One pipe can fill the pool in 9 hours. The second pipe can fill the pool in 6 hours. If both pipes were opened simultaneously, the pool could be filled in
   A. 3 hours, 36 minutes   B. 4 hours, 30 minutes
   C. 5 hours, 15 minutes   D. 7 hours, 30 minutes

130._____

131. John's father spent $4,800, which was one-fourth of his savings. He bought a car with three-eighths of the remainder of his savings His bank balance now amounts to
   A. $6,000   B. $6,400
   C. $9,000   D. $10,000

131._____

132. A clock that loses 4 minutes every 24 hours was set at 6 a.m. on October 1. What time was indicated by the clock when the correct time was 12:00 noon on October 6?
   A. 11:36 a.m.   B. 11:38 a.m.
   C. 11:39 a.m.   D. 11:40 a.m.

132._____

17 (#1)

133. A basketball team purchased uniforms from a sports shop for $268, less discounts of 15% and 10%. The check should be made out in the sum of
    A. $201.14
    B. $205.02
    C. $209.43
    D. None of the above

133._____

134. A secretary is entitled to 1-1/3 days of sick leave for every 32 days of work. How many days of work must the secretary have to her credit in order to be entitled to 12 days of sick leave?
    A. 272
    B. 288
    C. 290
    D. 512

134._____

135. A school secretary, whose annual salary is $10,980, contributes 9.8% to the Retirement Fund. Other monthly deductions from her salary are: federal income tax $140, state income tax $30, social security tax $20. The amount of her monthly check is
    A. $645.33
    B. $635.33
    C. $635.67
    D. $636.67

135._____

KEY (CORRECT ANSWERS)

1. A	31. C	61. B	91. A	121. D
2. D	32. B	62. C	92. C	122. A
3. C	33. C	63. D	93. B	123. D
4. D	34. D	64. D	94. C	124. B
5. A	35. A	65. D	95. C	125. C
6. A	36. C	66. C	96. B	126. A
7. B	37. B	67. D	97. D	127. A
8. A	38. D	68. B	98. A	128. B
9. B	39. C	69. B	99. B	129. C
10. B	40. B	70. D	100. D	130. B
11. C	41. D	71. D	101. C	131. C
12. B	42. B	72. C	102. B	132. D
13. A	43. B	73. C	103. D	133. D
14. D	44. C	74. D	104. B	134. B
15. C	45. B	75. B	105. B	135. B
16. C	46. C	76. B	106. D	
17. B	47. A	77. D	107. A	
18. A	48. C	78. D	108. A	
19. D	49. A	79. B	109. C	
20. D	50. D	80. C	110. B	
21. D	51. B	81. D	111. B	
22. C	52. B	82. C	112. A	
23. C	53. C	83. C	113. D	
24. A	54. D	84. A	114. A	
25. C	55. B	85. D	115. B	
26. D	56. C	86. C	116. C	
27. B	57. A	87. D	117. C	
28. D	58. D	88. A	118. B	
29. D	59. D	89. B	119. D	
30. A	60. C	90. A	120. A	

EXAMINATION SECTION
TEST 1

DIRECTIONS: Each question or incomplete statement is followed by several suggested answers or completions. Select the one that BEST answers the question or completes the statement. *PRINT THE LETTER OF THE CORRECT ANSWER IN THE SPACE AT THE RIGHT.*

1. The ∧ or caret symbol is a proofreader's mark which means that a 1.____
   A. space should have been left between two words
   B. new paragraph should be indicated
   C. word, phrase, or punctuation mark should be inserted
   D. word that is abbreviated should be spelled out

2. Of the following items, the one which should NOT be omitted from a typed inter-office memorandum is the 2.____
   A. salutation
   B. complementary closing
   C. formal signature
   D. names of those to receive copies

3. A typed rough draft should be double-spaced and should have wide margins PRIMARILY in order to 3.____
   A. save time in making typing corrections
   B. provide room for making insertions and corrections
   C. insure that the report is well-organized
   D. permit faster typing of the draft

4. In tabular reports, when a main heading, secondary heading, and single line of columnar headings are used, a triple space (2 blank lines) would be used after the _____ heading(s). 4.____
   A. main
   B. secondary
   C. columnar
   D. main and secondary

5. You have been requested to type a letter to Mr. Brown, a district attorney of a small town. 5.____
   Of the following, the CORRECT salutation to use is Dear
   A. District Attorney Brown:
   B. Mr. District Attorney:
   C. Mr. Brown:
   D. Honorable Brown:

6. A form letter that is sent to the public can be made to look more personal in appearance by doing all of the following EXCEPT 6.____
   A. using a meter stamp on the envelope of the letter
   B. having the letter signed with pen and ink
   C. using a good quality of paper for the letter
   D. matching the type used in the letter with that used for fill-ins

7. A senior typist opens a word-processing application to instruct a typist to create a table that contains three column headings. Under each column heading are three items.
Of the following, which sequence should the senior typist tell the typist to use when creating this table?
   A. First type the headings, and then type the items under them, a column at a time
   B. type each heading with its column of items under it, one column at a time
   C. first type the column of items, then center the headings above them
   D. type the headings and items across the page line by line

7.____

8. When a letter is addressed to an agency and a particular person should see it, an *attention line* is used.
This attention line is USUALLY found
   A. on the envelope only
   B. above the address
   C. below the address
   D. after the agency named in the address

8.____

9. The typing technique of *justifying* is used to
   A. decide how wide margins of different sized letters should be
   B. make all the lines of copy end evenly on the right-hand margin
   C. center headings above columns on tabular typed material
   D. condense the amount of space that is needed to make a manuscript look presentable

9.____

10. The date line on a letter is typed correctly when the date is ALL on one line
    A. with the month written out
    B. with slashes between the numbers
    C. and the month is abbreviated
    D. with a period at the end

10.____

11. When considering how wide to make a column when typing a table, the BASIC rule to follow is that the column should be as wide as the longest
    A. item in the body of the column
    B. heading of all of the columns
    C. item in the body or heading of that column
    D. heading or the longest item in the body of any column on that page

11.____

12. When a lengthy quotation is included in a letter or a report, it must be indicated that it is quoted material. This may be done by
    A. enclosing the quotation in parentheses
    B. placing an exclamation point at the end of the quotation
    C. using the apostrophe marks
    D. indenting from the regular margins on the left and right

12.____

13. In order to reach the highest rate of speed and the greatest degree of accuracy while typing, it is LEAST important to
    A. maintain good posture
    B. keep the hands and arms at a comfortable level
    C. strike the keys evenly
    D. keep the typing action in the wrists

14. It has been shown that the rate of typing and dictation drops when the secretary is not familiar with the language or topic of the copy.
    A practice that a supervisor might BEST advise to improve the knowledge and therefore increase the rate of typing dictation for such material would be for the secretary to
    A. plan a conference with her supervisor to discuss the subject matter
    B. read and review correspondence and related technical journals that come into the office
    C. recopy or retype previously transcribed material as practice
    D. withdraw sample materials from the files to take home for study

15. The one of the following in which the tab key is NOT generally used is the
    A. placement of the complimentary close and signature line
    B. indentation of paragraphs
    C. placement of the date line
    D. centering of title headings

16. In order for a business letter to be effective, it is LEAST important that it
    A. say what is meant simply and directly
    B. be written in formal language
    C. include all information the receiver needs to know
    D. be courteously written

17. If you are momentarily called away from your desk while typing a report of a confidential nature, you should cover or turn the copy over and
    A. remove the page being typed from the computer and file the report
    B. ask someone to watch your desk for you
    C. close the document so that the page is not visible
    D. spread a folder over the computer screen to conceal it

18. When typing a table that contains a column of figures and a column of words, the PROPER alignment of the column of figures and the column of words should be an even _____ the column of words.
    A. right-hand edge for the column of numbers and an even left-hand edge for
    B. right-hand edge for both the column of numbers and
    C. left-hand edge for the column of numbers and an even right-hand edge for
    D. left-hand edge for both the column of numbers and

19. The word *re*, when used in a memorandum, refers to the information that is on the _____ line.
    A. identification   B. subject   C. attention   D. reference

    19.____

20. Of the following uses of the period, the one which requires NO spacing after it when it is typed is when the period
    A. follows an abbreviation or an initial
    B. follows a figure or letter at the beginning of a line in a list of items
    C. comes between the initials that make up a single abbreviation
    D. comes at the end of a sentence

    20.____

21. This mark is a proofreader's mark meaning the word
    A. is misspelled
    B. should be underlined
    C. should be bold
    D. should be capitalized

    21.____

22. When typing a report that is double-spaced, the STANDARD recommended practice for indicating the start of new paragraphs is to
    A. double-space between paragraphs and indent the first word at least five spaces
    B. triple-space between paragraphs and indent the first word at least five spaces
    C. triple-space between paragraphs and type block style at the margin
    D. double-space between paragraphs and type block style at the margin

    22.____

23. In order to center a heading on a sheet of paper once the center of the paper has been found, the EASIEST and MOST efficient method to use is
    A. note the scale at each end of the heading to be centered and divide by two
    B. backspace from the center of the paper one space for every two letters and spaces in the heading
    C. arrange the heading around the middle number on the computer
    D. use a ruler to mark off the amount of space from both sides of the center of the paper that should be taken up by the heading

    23.____

24. You are about to type a single-spaced letter from a typewritten draft.
    In order to center this letter from top to bottom, your FIRST step should be to
    A. determine the number of spaces needed for the top and bottom margins
    B. determine the number of spaces needed for the left and right margins
    C. count the number of lines, including blank ones, which will be used for the letter
    D. subtract from the number of writing lines on the sheet of paper the number of lines that will not be used for the letter

    24.____

25. When typing a table which lists several amounts of money and the total in a column, the dollar sign should be placed in front of the
    A. first dollar amount only
    B. total dollar amount only
    C. first and total dollar amounts only
    D. all of the amounts of money in the column

    25.____

26. If a legal document is being prepared and requires necessary information to be typed into blank areas on preprinted legal forms, the margins for a line of typewritten material should be determined PRIMARILY by
    A. counting the total number of words to be typed
    B. the margins set for the pre-printed matter
    C. spacing backwards from the right margin rule
    D. the estimated width and height of the material to be entered

26.____

27. When checking for errors in material you've typed, it is BEST to
    A. proofread the material and use the spell-check function in combination
    B. give the material to someone else to review
    C. run the spell-check function and auto-correct all found errors
    D. proofread the material then e-mail it to another typist for final approval

27.____

28. Assume that Mr. Frank Foran is an acting official. In a letter written to him, the word *acting* would
    A. be used with the title in the address and in the salutation
    B. not be used with the title in the address
    C. be used with the title in the address but not in the salutation
    D. not be used with the title in the address or in the salutation

28.____

29. The software program that requires proficiency in typing in order to best utilize its MOST important features is
    A. Microsoft Excel   B. Adobe Reader
    C. Microsoft Word   D. Intuit QuickBooks

29.____

30. The MAIN reason for keeping a careful record of incoming mail is that
    A. greater speed and accuracy is obtained for answering outgoing mail
    B. this record is legal evidence
    C. it develops the efficiency of the office clerks
    D. the information may be useful some day

30.____

KEY (CORRECT ANSWERS)

1.	C	11.	C	21.	D
2.	D	12.	D	22.	A
3.	B	13.	D	23.	B
4.	B	14.	B	24.	C
5.	C	15.	D	25.	C
6.	A	16.	B	26.	B
7.	D	17.	C	27.	A
8.	C	18.	A	28.	C
9.	B	19.	B	29.	C
10.	A	20.	C	30.	A

TEST 2

DIRECTIONS: Each question or incomplete statement is followed by several suggested answers or completions. Select the one that BEST answers the question or completes the statement. *PRINT THE LETTER OF THE CORRECT ANSWER IN THE SPACE AT THE RIGHT.*

Questions 1-4.

DIRECTIONS: Questions 1 through 4 are to be answered SOLELY on the basis of the information contained in the following passage which is taken from a typing test.

Modern office methods, geared to ever higher speeds and aimed at ever greater efficiency, are largely the result of the typewriter. The typewriter is a substitute for handwriting; and, in the hands of a skilled typist, not only turns out letters and other documents at least three times faster than a penman can do the work, but turns out the greater volume more uniformly and legibly. With the use of carbon paper and onionskin paper, identical copies can be made at the same time.

The typewriter, besides its effect on the conduct of business and government, has had a very important effect on the position of women. The typewriter has done much to bring women into business and government, and today there are vastly more women than men typists. Many women have used the keys of the typewriter to climb the ladder to responsible managerial positions.

The typewriter, as its name implies, employs type to make an ink impression on paper. For many years, the manual typewriter was the standard machine used. Today, the electric typewriter is dominant, with electronic typewriters, word processors, and computers coming into wider use.

The mechanism of the office manual typewriter includes a set of keys arranged systematically in rows; a semicircular frame of type, connected to the keys by levers; the carriage or paper carrier; a rubber roller called a platen, against which the type strikes; and an inked ribbon which makes the impression of the type character when the key strikes it. This machine, once omnipresent, is an antique today.

1. The above passage mentions a number of good features of the combination of a skilled typist and a typewriter.
   Of the following, the feature which is NOT mentioned in the passage is
   A. speed   B. uniformity   C. reliability   D. legibility

   1.____

2. According to the above passage, a skilled typist can
   A. turn out at least five carbon copies of typed matter
   B. type at least three times faster than a penman can write
   C. type more than 80 words a minute
   D. readily move into a managerial position

   2.____

49

3. According to the above passage, which of the following is NOT part of the mechanism of a manual typewriter?   3.____
   A. Carbon paper B. Paper carrier
   C. Platen D. Inked ribbon

4. According to the above passage, the typewriter has helped   4.____
   A. men more than women in business
   B. women in career advancement into management
   C. men and women equally, but women have taken better advantage of it
   D. more women than men, because men generally dislike routine typing work

5. Standard rules for typing spacing have developed through usage. According to these rules, two spaces are left after a(n)   5.____
   A. colon B. comma
   C. hyphen D. opening parenthesis

6. Assume that you have to type the heading CENTERING TYPED HEADINGS on a piece of paper which extends from 0 to 100 on the typewriter scale. You want the heading to be perfectly centered on the paper.   6.____
   In order to find the proper point on the typewriter scale at which to begin typing, you should determine the paper's center point on the typewriter scale and then _____ the number of letters and spaces in the heading.
   A. add B. add one-half
   C. subtract D. subtract one-half

7. While typing from a rough draft, the practice of reading a line ahead of what you are now typing is considered to be a   7.____
   A. *good* practice; it may prepare your fingers for the words which you will be typing
   B. *good* practice; it may help you to review the subject matter contained in the material
   C. *poor* practice; it may increase your typing speed so that your accuracy is decreased
   D. *poor* practice; it may cause you to lose your concentration and make errors in the words you are presently typing

8. Assume that you are transcribing a letter and you are not sure how to divide a word at the end of a line you are typing.   8.____
   The BEST way to determine where to divide the word is by
   A. asking your supervisor
   B. asking the person who dictated the letter
   C. checking with other stenographers
   D. looking up the word in a dictionary

9. When taking proper care of a typewriter, it is NOT a desirable action to
    A. clean the feed rolls with a cloth
    B. dust the exterior surface of the machine
    C. oil the rubber parts of the machine
    D. use a type-cleaning brush to clean the keys

10. Of the following, the LEAST desirable action to take when typing a rough draft of a report is to
    A. cross out typing errors instead of erasing them
    B. double or triple space between lines
    C. provide large margins on all sides of the typing paper
    D. use letterhead or onionskin paper

11. The date line of every business letter should indicate the month, the day of the month, and the year.
    The MOST common practice when typing a date line is to type it as
    A. Jan. 12, 2018
    B. January 12, 2018
    C. 1-12-18
    D. 1/12/18

Questions 12-16.

DIRECTIONS: Questions 12 through 16 are to be answered SOLELY on the basis of the information provided in the following passage.

A written report is a communication of information from one person to another. It is an account of some matter especially investigated, however routine that matter may be. The ultimate basis of any good written report is facts, which became known through observation and verification. Good written reports may seem to be no more than general ideas and opinions. However, in such cases, the facts leading to these opinions were gathered, verified, and reported earlier, and the opinions are dependent upon these facts. Good style, proper form, and emphasis cannot make a good written report out of unreliable information and bad judgments but on the other hand, solid investigation and brilliant thinking are not likely to become very useful until they are effectively communicated to others. If a person's work calls for written reports, then his work is often no better than his written reports.

12. Based on the information in the above passage, it can be concluded that opinions expressed in a report should be
    A. based on facts which are gathered and reported
    B. emphasized repeatedly when they result from a special investigation
    C. kept to a minimum
    D. separated from the body of the report

13. In the above passage, the one of the following which is mentioned as a way of establishing facts is
    A. authority
    B. communication
    C. reporting
    D. verification

4 (#2)

14. According to the above passage, the characteristic shared by ALL written reports is that they are
    A. accounts of routine matters
    B. transmissions of information
    C. reliable and logical
    D. written in proper form

14.____

15. Which of the following conclusions can LOGICALLY be drawn from the information given in the above passage?
    A. Brilliant thinking can make up for unreliable information in a report.
    B. One method of judging an individual's work is the quality of the written reports he is required to submit.
    C. Proper form and emphasis can make a good report out of unreliable information.
    D. Good written reports that seem to be no more than general ideas should be rewritten.

15.____

16. Which of the following suggested titles would be MOST appropriate for this passage?
    A. GATHERING AND ORGANIZING FACTS
    B. TECHNIQUES OF OBSERVATION
    C. NATURE AND PURPOSE OF REPORTS
    D. REPORTS AND OPINIONS: DIFFERENCES AND SIMILARITIES

16.____

Questions 17-25

DIRECTIONS: Each of Questions 17 through 25 consists of a sentence which may or may not be an example of good English usage. Examine each sentence, considering grammar, punctuation, spelling, capitalization, and awkwardness. Then choose the correct statement about it from the four choices below it. If the English usage in the sentence given is better than any of the changes suggested in Choices B, C, or D, pick choice A. Do NOT pick a choice that will change the meaning of the sentence.

17. We attended a staff conference on Wednesday the new safety and fire rules were discussed.
    A. This is an example of acceptable writing.
    B. The words *safety*, *fire*, and *rules* should begin with capital letters.
    C. There should be a comma after the word *Wednesday*.
    D. There should be a period after the word *Wednesday*, and the word *the* should begin with a capital letter.

17.____

18. Neither the dictionary or the telephone directory could be found in the office library.
    A. This is an example of acceptable writing.
    B. The word *or* should be changed to *nor*.
    C. The word *library* should be spelled *libery*.
    D. The word *neither* should be changed to *either*.

18.____

19. The report would have been typed correctly if the typist cold read the draft.   19.____
    A. This is an example of acceptable writing.
    B. The word *would* should be removed.
    C. The word *have* should be inserted after the word *could*.
    D. The word *correctly* should be changed to *correct*.

20. The supervisor brought the reports and forms to an employees desk.   20.____
    A. This is an example of acceptable writing.
    B. The word *brought* should be changed to *took*.
    C. There should be a comma after the word *reports* and a comma after the word *forms*.
    D. The word *employees* should be spelled *employee's*.

21. It's important for all the office personnel to submit their vacation schedules on time.   21.____
    A. This is an example of acceptable writing.
    B. The word *It's* should be spelled *Its*.
    C. The word *their* should be spelled *they're*.
    D. The word *personnel* should be spelled *personal*.

22. The supervisor wants that all staff members report to the office at 9:00 A.M.   22.____
    A. This is an example of acceptable writing.
    B. The word *that* should be removed and the word *to* should be inserted after the word *members*.
    C. There should be a comma after the word *wants* and a comma after the word *office*.
    D. The word *wants* should be changed to *want* and the word *shall* should be inserted after the word *members*.

23. Every morning the clerk opens the office mail and distributes it.   23.____
    A. This is an example of acceptable writing.
    B. The word *opens* should be changed to *open*.
    C. The word *mail* should be changed to *letters*.
    D. The word *it* should be changed to *them*.

24. The secretary typed more fast on an electric typewriter than on a manual typewriter.   24.____
    A. This is an example of acceptable writing.
    B. The words *more fast* should be changed to *faster*.
    C. There should be a comma after the words *electric typewriter*.
    D. The word *than* should be changed to *then*.

25. The new stenographer needed a desk a typewriter, a chair and a blotter.   25.____
    A. This is an example of acceptable writing.
    B. The word *blotter* should be spelled *blodder*.
    C. The word *stenographer* should begin with a capital letter.
    D. There should be a comma after the word *desk*.

KEY (CORRECT ANSWERS)

1.	C	11.	B
2.	B	12	A
3.	A	13.	D
4.	B	14.	B
5.	A	15.	B
6.	D	16.	C
7.	D	17.	D
8.	D	18.	B
9.	C	19.	C
10.	D	20.	D

21. A
22. B
23. A
24. B
25. D

EXAMINATION SECTION
TEST 1

DIRECTIONS: Each question or incomplete statement is followed by several suggested answers or completions. Select the one that BEST answers the question or completes the statement. *PRINT THE LETTER OF THE CORRECT ANSWER IN THE SPACE AT THE RIGHT.*

1. Which of the following is the acceptable format for typing the date line?   1.____
   - A. 12/2/16
   - B. December 2, 2016
   - C. December 2nd, 2016
   - D. Dec. 2 2016

2. When typing a letter, which of the following is INACCURATE?   2.____
   - A. If the letter is to be more than one page long, subsequent sheets should be blank, but should match the letterhead sheet in size, color, weight, and texture.
   - B. Long quoted material must be centered and single-spaced internally.
   - C. Quotation marks must be used when there is long quoted material.
   - D. Double spacing is used above and below tables and long quotations to set them off from the rest of the material.

3. Which of the following is INACCURATE?   3.____
   - A. When an addressee's title in an inside address would overrun the center of a page, it's best to carry part of the title over to another line and to indent it by two spaces.
   - B. It is permissible to use ordinal numbers in an inside address.
   - C. In addresses involving street numbers under three, the number is written out in full.
   - D. In the inside address, suite, apartment or room numbers should be placed on the line after the street address.

4. All of the following are common styles of business letters EXCEPT   4.____
   - A. simplified
   - B. block
   - C. direct
   - D. executive

5. Please select the two choices below that correctly represent how a continuation sheet heading may be typed.   5.____
   - I. Page 2
      Mr. Alan Post
      June 25, 2016
   - II. Page 2
      Mr. Alan Post
      6-25-16
   - III. Mr. Alan Post   -2-
      June 25, 2016
   - IV. Mr. Alan Post   -2-
      6-25-16

   The CORRECT answer is:
   - A. I, II
   - B. II, III
   - C. I, III
   - D. II, IV

6. Which of the following is INCORRECT? It is   6.____
   - A. permissible to abbreviate honorifics in the inside address
   - B. permissible to abbreviate company or organizational names, departmental designations, or organizational titles in the inside address

2 (#1)

C. permissible to use abbreviations in the inside address if they have been used on the printed letterhead and form part of the official company name
D. sometimes permissible to omit the colon after the salutation

7. Which of the following is INCORRECT? 7.____

   A. The subject line of a letter gives the main idea of the message as succinctly as possible.
   B. If a letter contains an enclosure, there should be a notation indicating this.
   C. Important enclosures ought to be listed numerically and described.
   D. An enclosure notation should be typed flush with the right margin.

8. Which of the following is INACCURATE about inside addresses? 8.____

   A. An intraoffice or intracompany mail stop number such as DA 3C 61B is put after the organization or company name with at least two spaces intervening.
   B. Words such as *Avenue* should not be abbreviated.
   C. With the exception of runovers, the inside address should not be more than five full lines.
   D. The inside address includes the recipient's courtesy or honorific title and his or her full name on line one; the recipient's title on the next line; the recipient's official organizational affiliation on the next line; the street address on the penultimate line; and the city, state, and zip code on the last line.

9. Which of the following is an INCORRECT example of how to copy recipients when using copy notation? 9.____

   A. cc: Martin A.Sheen
   B. cc: Ms. Connors
           Ms. Grogan
           Ms. Reynolds
   C. CC: Martin A. Sheen
   D. cc: Mr. Right
           Mr. Wrong
           Mr. Perfect

10. When typing a memo, all of the following are true EXCEPT 10.____

    A. it is permissible to use an abbreviation like 1/1/16
    B. the subject line should be underlined
    C. titles such as *Mr.* or *Dr.* are usually not used on the *To* line
    D. unless the memo is very short, paragraphs should be single-spaced and double spacing should be used to separate the paragraphs from each other

11. When typing a letter, which of the following is INACCURATE? 11.____

    A. Paragraphs in business letters are usually single-spaced, with double spacing separating them from each other.
    B. Margin settings used on subsequent sheets should match those used on the letterhead sheet.
    C. If the message contains an enumerated list, it is best to block and center the listed material by five or six more spaces, right and left.
    D. A quotation of more than three typed lines must be single-spaced and centered on the page.

12. A letter that is to be signed by Hazel Alice Putney, but written by Mary Jane Roberts, and typed by Alice Carol Bell would CORRECTLY bear the following set of initials:

    A. HAP:MJR:acb
    B. HAP:MJR:ab
    C. HAP:mjr:acb
    D. HAP:mjr:ab

13. Which of the following is INCORRECT?

    A. My dear Dr. Jones:
    B. Dear Accounting Department:
    C. Dear Dr. Jones:
    D. Dear Mr. Al Lee, Esq.:

14. Which of the following is INCORRECT?

    A. Bcc stands for blind copy or blind courtesy copy.
    B. When a blind copy is used, the notation bcc appears only on the original.
    C. When a blind copy is used, the notation may appear in the top left corner of the letterhead sheet.
    D. If following a letter style that uses indented paragraphs, the postscript should be indented in exactly the same manner.

15. All of the following are true of the complimentary close EXCEPT

    A. it is typed two lines beneath the last line of the message
    B. when using a minimal punctuation system, you may omit the comma in the complimentary close if you have used a colon in the salutation
    C. where the complimentary close is placed may vary
    D. the first word of the complimentary close is capitalized

16. When typing a letter, which of the following is INACCURATE?

    A. Tables should be centered.
    B. If the letter is to be more than one page long, at least three lines of the message itself should be carried over.
    C. The message begins two lines below the salutation in almost all letter styles.
    D. Triple spacing should be used above and below lists to set them off from the rest of the letter.

17. Which one of the following is INCORRECT?

    A. When used, special mailing instructions should be indicated on both the envelope and the letter itself.
    B. Depending upon the length of the message and the available space, special mailing instructions are usually typed flush left, about four spaces below the date line and about two lines above the first line of the inside address.
    C. Certification, registration, special delivery, and overseas air mail are all considered special mailing instructions.
    D. Special mailing instructions should not be typed in capital letters.

18. Which of the following is INCORRECT?

    A. When a letter is intended to be personal or confidential, these instructions are typewritten in capital letters on the envelope and on the letter itself.

B. When a letter is intended to be personal or confidential, these instructions are typewritten in capital letters on the envelope, but not on the letter.
C. A letter marked PERSONAL is an eyes-only communication for the recipient.
D. A letter marked CONFIDENTIAL means that the recipient and any other authorized person may open and read it.

19. All of the following are true in regard to copy notation EXCEPT

    A. when included in a letter, a copy notation should be typed flush with the left margin, two lines below the signature block or two lines below any preceding notation
    B. copy notation should appear after writer/typist initials and/or enclosure notations, if these are used
    C. the copy recipient's full name and address should be indicated
    D. if more than one individual is to be copied, recipients should be listed in alphabetical order according to full name or initials

19.____

20. When addressing envelopes, which of the following is INACCURATE?

    A. When both street address and box number are used, the destination of the letter should be placed on the line just above the city, state, and zip code line.
    B. Special mailing instructions are typed in capital letters below the postage.
    C. Special handling instructions should be typed in capital letters and underlined.
    D. The address should be single-spaced.

20.____

21. All of the following should be capitalized EXCEPT the

    A. first word of a direct quotation
    B. first word in the continuation of a split, single-sentence quotation
    C. names of organizations
    D. names of places and geographic districts, regions, divisions, and locales

21.____

22. All of the following are true about capitalization EXCEPT

    A. words indicating direction and regions are capitalized
    B. the names of rivers, seas, lakes, mountains, and oceans are capitalized
    C. the names of nationalities, tribes, languages, and races are capitalized
    D. civil, military, corporate, royal and noble, honorary, and religious titles are capitalized when they precede a name

22.____

23. All of the following are true about capitalization EXCEPT

    A. key words in the titles of musical, dramatic, artistic, and literary works are capitalized as are the first and last words
    B. the first word of the salutation and of the complimentary close of a letter is capitalized
    C. abbreviations and acronyms are not capitalized
    D. the days of the week, months of the year, holidays, and holy days are capitalized

23.____

24. All of the following are true EXCEPT

    A. an apostrophe indicates the omission of letters in contractions
    B. an apostrophe indicates the possessive case of singular and plural nouns

24.____

C. an apostrophe should not be used to indicate the omission of figures in dates
D. ellipses are used to indicate the omission of words or sentences within quoted material

25. All of the following are true EXCEPT

    A. brackets may be used to enclose words or passages in quotations to indicate the insertion of material written by someone other than the original writer
    B. brackets may be used to enclose material that is inserted within material already in parentheses
    C. a dash, rather than a colon, should be used to introduce a list
    D. a colon may be used to introduce a long quotation

26. All of the following are true EXCEPT a(n)

    A. comma may be used to set off short quotations and sayings
    B. apostrophe is often used to represent the word *per*
    C. dash may be used to indicate a sudden change or break in continuity
    D. dash may be used to set apart an emphatic or defining phrase

27. All of the following are true EXCEPT

    A. a hyphen may be used as a substitute for the word *to* between figures or words
    B. parentheses are used to enclose material that is not an essential part of the sentence and that, if not included, would not change its meaning
    C. single quotation marks are used to enclose quotations within quotations
    D. semicolons and colons are put inside closing quotation marks

28. All of the following are true EXCEPT

    A. commas and periods should be put inside closing quotation marks
    B. for dramatic effect, a semicolon may be used instead of a comma to signal longer pauses
    C. a semicolon is used to set off city and state in geographic names
    D. italics are used to represent the titles of magazines and newspapers

29. According to standard rules for typing, two spaces are left after a

    A. closing parenthesis   B. comma
    C. number   D. colon

30. All of the following are true EXCEPT

    A. rounding out large numbers is often acceptable
    B. it is best to use numerical figures to express specific hours, measures, dates, page numbers, coordinates, and addresses
    C. when a sentence begins with a number, it is best to use numerical figures rather than to spell the number out
    D. when two or more numbers appear in one sentence, it is best to spell them out consistently or use numerical figures consistently, regardless of the size of the numbers

31. All of the following are true about word division EXCEPT

    A. words should not be divided on a single letter
    B. it is acceptable to carry over two-letter endings
    C. the final word in a paragraph should not be divided
    D. words in headings should not be divided

32. All of the following are true of word division EXCEPT

    A. it is preferable to divide words of three or more syllables after the consonant
    B. it is best to avoid breaking words on more than two consecutive lines
    C. words should be divided according to pronunciation
    D. two-syllable words are divided at the end of the first syllable

33. All of the following are true of word division EXCEPT

    A. words with short prefixes should be divided after the prefix
    B. prefixes and combining forms of more than one syllable should be divided after the first syllable
    C. the following word endings are not divided: -gion, -gious, -sial, -sion, -tial, -tion, -tious, -ceous, -cial, -cient, -cion, -cious, and -geous
    D. words ending in -er should not be divided if the division could only occur on the -er form

34. All of the following are true about word division EXCEPT

    A. words should be divided so that the part of the word left at the end of the line will suggest the word
    B. abbreviations should not be divided
    C. the suffixes -able and -ible are usually divided instead of being carried over intact to the next line
    D. when the addition of -ed, -est, -er, or a similar ending causes the doubling of a final consonant, the added consonant is carried over

35. All of the following are true of word division EXCEPT

    A. words with doubled consonants are usually divided between those consonants
    B. it is permissible to divide contractions
    C. words of one syllable should not be split
    D. it is best to try to avoid divisions that add a hyphen to an already hyphenated word

36. All of the following are true of word division EXCEPT

    A. dividing proper names should be avoided wherever possible
    B. two consonants, preceded and followed by a vowel, are divided after the first consonant
    C. even though two adjoining vowels are sounded separately, it is best not to divide between the two vowels
    D. it is best not to divide the month and day when typing dates, but the year may be carried over to the next line

37. Which of the following four statements are CORRECT? It would be acceptable to divide the word
    I. *organization* after the first *a* in the word
    II. *recommend* after the first *m*
    III. *interface* between the *r* and the *f*
    IV. *development* between the *e* and the *l*
    The CORRECT answer is:

    A. I *only*   B. II, III
    C. II *only*   D. I, II, III

38. Which of the following is divided INCORRECTLY?

    A. usu-ally   B. call-ing
    C. pro-blem   D. micro-computer

39. Which of the following is divided INCORRECTLY?

    A. imag-inary   B. commun-ity
    C. manage-able   D. commun-ion

40. Which of the following is divided INCORRECTLY?

    A. spa-ghetti   B. retro-spective
    C. proof-reader D. fix-ed

41. Which of the following is divided INCORRECTLY?

    A. Mr. Han-rahan B. control-lable
    C. pro-jectile   D. proj-ect

42. Which of the following is divided INCORRECTLY?

    A. prom-ise   B. han-dling
    C. have-n't   D. pro-duce

43. Which of the following is divided INCORRECTLY?

    A. ship-ped   B. audi-ble
    C. hypo-crite   D. refer-ring

44. Which of the following is divided INCORRECTLY?

    A. particu-lar   B. spac-ious
    C. chang-ing   D. capac-ity

45. There is a critical need to develop the ability to control the mind, especailly the ability to stop repeating negative thoughts. Often, when we must swallow our anger, we are left running an enless tape of thoughts. We can't stop thinking about what the person said and what we should have said in response. To combat this tendency, it is helpful to practice witnessing our thoughts. If we can remain detached from them, we won't fuel them, and they will just run out of gas. As we watch them, we also learn a lot about ourselves. The catch here is not to judge them. Judging may lead to selfblaming, blaming others, excuses, rationalizations, and other thoughts that just add fuel. Another technique is is substituting positive thoughts for negative ones.

It is difficult to do this in the "heat of the moment". With practice, however, its possible
to train the mind to do what we want it to do and to contain what we want it to contain.
A mind is like a garden – we can weed it, or we can let it grow wild.
The above paragraph contains a number of typographical errors.
How many lines in this paragraph contain typographical errors?

   A. 5   B. 6   C. 8   D. 9

KEY (CORRECT ANSWERS)

1. B	11. D	21. B	31. B	41. A
2. C	12. A	22. A	32. A	42. A
3. D	13. D	23. C	33. B	43. A
4. C	14. B	24. C	34. C	44. B
5. C	15. B	25. C	35. B	45. C
6. B	16. D	26. B	36. C	
7. D	17. D	27. D	37. B	
8. B	18. B	28. C	38. C	
9. D	19. C	29. D	39. B	
10. B	20. C	30. C	40. D	

TEST 2

DIRECTIONS: Each sentence may or may not contain problems in capitalization or punctuation. If there is an error, select the number of the underlined part that must be changed to make the sentence correct. If the sentence has no error, select choice E. **No sentence contains more than one error.**

1. Is the choice for <u>P</u>resident of the company <u>George Dawson</u> or Marilyn <u>Kappel?</u> <u>No error</u>
                 A   B   C   D   E

2. "To tell you the truth<u>,</u> I was really <u>disappointed</u> that our <u>F</u>all percentages did not show more sales growth<u>,</u>" remarked the bookkeeper. <u>No error</u>
                        A   B   C   D   E

3. Bruce gave his <u>U</u>ncle clear directions to go <u>s</u>outh on Maplewood Drive<u>,</u> turn left at the intersection with Birch Lane, and then proceed for two miles until he reached Columbia <u>County</u>. <u>No error</u>
                    A   B   C   D   E

4. Janet hopes to transfer to a <u>c</u>ollege in the <u>e</u>ast <u>d</u>uring her <u>j</u>unior year. <u>No error</u>
                                    A   B C   D   E

5. The <u>D</u>eclaration <u>o</u>f Independence states<u>_</u> that we have the right to the pursuit of <u>H</u>appiness, but it doesn't guarantee that we'll ever find it. <u>No error</u>
        A   B   C   D   E

6. We campaigned hard for the <u>m</u>ayor<u>,</u> but we<u>'</u>re still not sure if he'll win against <u>S</u>enator Frankovich. <u>No error</u>
                                  A   B   C   D   E

7. Mr. <u>Butler's</u> <u>F</u>ord was parked right behind <u>our's</u> on Atlantic <u>Avenue</u>. <u>No error</u>
            A   B   C   D   E

8. "<u>I</u> respect your <u>opinion,</u> but I cannot agree with <u>it."</u> commented my <u>g</u>randmother. <u>No error</u>
      A   B   C   D   E

9. My friends, of course, were surprised when when I did so well on the Math section
         A   B   C   D
   of the test. No error
                 E

10. Dr. Vogel and Senator Rydell decided that the meeting would be held on February 6,
                    A   B   C
    in Ithaca, New York. No error
        D   E

11. "Frank, do you understand what we're telling you?" asked the doctor. No error
        A   B   C   D   E

12. When I asked my daughter what she knew about politics, she claimed she
                    A   B   C
    knew nothing. No error
           D   E

13. "If you went to my high school, dad, you'd see things differently," snapped Sean.
                      A A   B C   D
    No error
      E

14. In Carlos' third year of high school, he took geometry, psychology, french, and chemis-
        A   B B   C   D
    try. No error
        E

15. "When you enter the building," the guard instructed us, "turn left down the long, wind-
                               A   B C   D
    ing corridor." No error
                 E

16. We hope to spend a weekend in the Catskill Mountains in the spring, and we'd like to
                                        A   B C   D
    go to Florida in January. No error
                                E

17. A clerk in the department of Justice asked Carol and me if we were there on business or
      A   B   C
    just sight-seeing. No error
               D   E

18. Jamie joined a cult, Harry's in a rock band, and Carol-Ann is studying chinese literature
       A   B   C
    at the University of Southern California. No error
             D   E

19. Parker Flash asked if my band had ever played at the
                   A
    Purple Turnip, a club in Orinoco Hills. No error
    B   C   D   E

20. "The gift of the Magi" is a short story by O'Henry that deals with the sad ironies of life.
         A B C   D
    No error
    E

21. Darwin's theory was developed, as a result of his trip to the Galapagos Islands.
        A B   C   D
    No error
    E

22. Is 10 Downing street the address of Sherlock Holmes or the British Prime Minister?
           A   B   C   D
    No error
    E

23. While President Johnson was in Office, his Great Society program passed a great deal
              A   B   C   D
    of important legislation. No error
                              E

24. If, as the American Industrial Health Council's study says, one out of every five can-
        A   B   C
    cers today is caused by the workplace, it is a tragic indictment of what is happening
                                D
    there. No error
           E

25. According to the Articles of Confederation, Congress could issue money, but it could
                              A   B   C
    not prevent States from issuing their own money. No error
                   D   E

26. "I'd really like to know whos going to be shoveling the driveway this winter," said
                        A   B   C   D
    Laverne. No error
             ‾‾‾‾‾‾‾‾
                E

27. According to Carl Jung the Swiss psychologist, playing with fantasy is the key to cre-
                      A   B   C   D
    ativity. No error
            ‾‾‾‾‾‾‾‾
               E

28. Don't you find it odd that people would prefer jumping A off the Golden Gate bridge to
        A   B
    jumping off other bridges in the area ?   No error
                                    C   D   ‾‾‾‾‾‾‾‾
                                                E

29. While driving through the South, we saw many of the sites of famous Civil war battles. .
                                A B   C   D
    No error
    ‾‾‾‾‾‾‾‾
       E

30. Although I have always valued my Grandmother's china, I prefer her collection
                                          A   B   C
    of South American art. No error
       D   ‾‾‾‾‾‾‾‾
                             E

KEY (CORRECT ANSWERS)

1.	A	16.	E
2.	C	17.	B
3.	A	18.	C
4.	B	19.	C
5.	D	20.	A
6.	E	21.	C
7.	C	22.	B
8.	E	23.	B
9.	D	24.	D
10.	E	25.	D
11.	A	26.	B
12.	B	27.	A
13.	C	28.	B
14.	D	29.	C
15.	E	30.	A

EXAMINATION SECTION
TEST 1

DIRECTIONS: Each question or incomplete statement is followed by several suggested answers or completions. Select the one that BEST answers the question or completes the statement. *PRINT THE LETTER OF THE CORRECT ANSWER IN THE SPACE AT THE RIGHT.*

Questions 1-10.

WORD MEANING

DIRECTIONS: Each question from 1 to 10 contains a word in capitals followed by four suggested meanings of the word. For each question, choose the best meaning. *PRINT THE LETTER OF THE CORRECT ANSWER IN THE SPACE AT THE RIGHT.*

1. ACCURATE   1.____
   A. correct   B. useful   C. afraid   D. careless

2. ALTER   2.____
   A. copy   B. change   C. report   D. agree

3. DOCUMENT   3.____
   A. outline   B. agreement   C. blueprint   D. record

4. INDICATE   4.____
   A. listen   B. show   C. guess   D. try

5. INVENTORY   5.____
   A. custom   B. discovery   C. warning   D. list

6. ISSUE   6.____
   A. annoy   B. use up   C. give out   D. gain

7. NOTIFY   7.____
   A. inform   B. promise   C. approve   D. strengthen

8. ROUTINE   8.____
   A. path   B. mistake   C. habit   D. journey

9. TERMINATE   9.____
   A. rest   B. start   C. deny   D. end

10. TRANSMIT   10.____
    A. put in   B. send   C. stop   D. go across

Questions 11-15.

READING COMPREHENSION

DIRECTIONS: Questions 11 through 15 test how well you understand what you read. It will be necessary for you to read carefully because your answers to these questions should be based ONLY on the information given in the following paragraphs.

The recipient gains an impression of a typewritten letter before he begins to read the message. Pastors which provide for a good first impression include margins and spacing that are visually pleasing, formal parts of the letter which are correctly placed according to the style of the letter, copy which is free of obvious erasures and over-strikes, and transcript that is even and clear. The problem for the typist is that of how to produce that first, positive impression of her work.

There are several general rules which a typist can follow when she wishes to prepare a properly spaced letter on a sheet of letter-head. Ordinarily, the width of a letter should not be less than four inches nor more than six inches. The side margins should also have a desirable relation to the bottom margin and the space between the letterhead and the body of the letter. Usually the most appealing arrangement is when the side margins are even and the bottom margin is slightly wider than the side margins. In some offices, however, standard line length is used for all business letters, and the secretary then varies the spacing between the date line and the inside address according to the length of the letter.

11. The BEST title for the above paragraphs would be: 11._____

    A. Writing Office Letters
    B. Making Good First Impressions
    C. Judging Well-Typed Letters
    D. Good Placing and Spacing for Office Letters

12. According to the above paragraphs, which of the following might be considered the way   12._____
    in which people very quickly judge the quality of work which has been typed? By

    A. measuring the margins to see if they are correct
    B. looking at the spacing and cleanliness of the typescript
    C. scanning the body of the letter for meaning
    D. reading the date line and address for errors

13. What, according to the above paragraphs, would be definitely UNDESIRABLE as the   13._____
    average line length of a typed letter?

    A. 4"   B. 5"   C. 6"   D. 7"

14. According to the above paragraphs, when the line length is kept standard, the secretary   14._____

    A. does not have to vary the spacing at all since this also is standard
    B. adjusts the spacing between the date line and inside address for different lengths of letters
    C. uses the longest line as a guideline for spacing between the date line and inside address
    D. varies the number of spaces between the lines

15. According to the above paragraphs, side margins are MOST pleasing when they   15.____
    A. are even and somewhat smaller than the bottom margin
    B. are slightly wider than the bottom margin
    C. vary with the length of the letter
    D. are figured independently from the letterhead and the body of the letter

Questions 16-20.

CODING

DIRECTIONS:

```
Name of Applicant    H A N G S B R U K E
Test Code            c o m p l e x i t y
File Number          0 1 2 3 4 5 6 7 8 9
```

Assume that each of the above capital letters is the first letter of the name of an Applicant, that the small letter directly beneath each capital letter is the test code for the Applicant, and that the number directly beneath each code letter is the file number for the Applicant.

In each of the following Questions 16 through 20, the test code letters and the file numbers in Columns 2 and 3 should correspond to the capital letters in Column 1. For each question, look at each column carefully and mark your answer as follows:

If there is an error only in Column 2, mark your answer A.
If there is an error only in Column 3, mark your answer B.
If there is an error in both Columns 2 and 3, mark your answer C.
If both Columns 2 and 3 are correct, mark your answer D.

The following sample question is given to help you understand the procedure.

SAMPLE QUESTION

Column 1	Column 2	Column 3
AKEHN	otyci	18902

In Column 2, the final test code letter *i.* should be *m*. Column 3 is correctly coded to Column 1. Since there is an error only in Column 2, the answer is A.

	Column 1	Column 2	Column 3	
16.	NEKKU	mytti	29987	16.____
17.	KRAEB	txyle	86095	17.____
18.	ENAUK	ymoit	92178	18.____
19.	REANA	xeomo	69121	19.____
20.	EKHSE	ytcxy	97049	20.____

Questions 21-30.

ARITHMETICAL REASONING

21. If a secretary answered 28 phone calls and typed the addresses for 112 credit statements in one morning, what is the ratio of phone calls answered to credit statements typed for that period of time?

    A. 1:4 B. 1:7 C. 2:3 D. 3:5

    21._____

22. According to a suggested filing system, no more than 10 folders should be filed behind any one file guide and from 15 to 25 file guides should be used in each file drawer for easy finding and filing.
    The maximum number of folders that a five-drawer file cabinet can hold to allow easy finding and filing is

    A. 550 B. 750 C. 1,100 D. 1,250

    22._____

23. An employee had a starting salary of $25,804. He received a salary increase at the end of each year, and at the end of the seventh year his salary was $33,476.
    What was his average annual increase in salary over these seven years?

    A. $1,020 B. $1,076 C. $1,096 D. $1,144

    23._____

24. The 55 typists and 28 senior clerks in a certain city agency were paid a total of $1,943,200 in salaries last year.
    If the average annual salary of a typist was $22,400 the average annual salary of a senior clerk was

    A. $25,400 B. $26,600 C. $26,800 D. $27,000

    24._____

25. A typist has been given a three page report to type. She has finished typing the first two pages. The first page has 283 words, and the second page has 366 words.
    If the total report consists of 954 words, how many words will she have to type on the third page of the report?

    A. 202 B. 287 C. 305 D. 313

    25._____

26. In one day, Clerk A processed 30% more forms than Clerk B, and Clerk C processed Ii times as many forms as Clerk A. If Clerk B processed 40 forms, how many more forms were processed by Clerk C than Clerk B?

    A. 12 B. 13 C. 21 D. 25

    26._____

27. A clerk who earns a gross salary of $452 every two weeks has the following deductions taken from her paycheck:
    15% for City, State, Federal taxes; 2 1/2% for Social Security; $1.30 for health insurance; and $6.00 for union dues. The amount of her take-home pay is

    A. $256.20 B. $312.40 C. $331.60 D. $365.60

    27._____

28. In 2005, a city agency spent $2,000 to buy pencils at a cost of $5.00 a dozen.
    If the agency used 3/4 of these pencils in 2005 and used the same number of pencils in 2006, how many more pencils did it have to buy to have enough pencils for all of 2006?

    A. 1,200 B. 2,400 C. 3,600 D. 4,800

    28._____

29. A clerk who worked in Agency X earned the following salaries: $20,140 the first year, $21,000 the second year, and $21,920 the third year. Another clerk who worked in Agency Y for three years earned $21,100 a year for two years and $21,448 the third year. The difference between the average salaries received by both clerks over a three-year period is

    A. $196　　B. $204　　C. $348　　D. $564

30. An employee who works over 40 hours in any week receives overtime payment for the extra hours at time and one-half (1 1/2 times) his hourly rate of pay. An employee who earns $13.60 an hour works a total of 45 hours during a certain week.
    His total pay for that week would be

    A. $564.40　　B. $612.00　　C. $646.00　　D. $812.00

Questions 31-35.

RELATED INFORMATION

31. To tell a newly-employed clerk to fill a top drawer of a four-drawer cabinet with heavy folders which will be often used and to keep lower drawers only partly filled is

    A. *good,* because a tall person would have to bend unnecessarily if he had to use a lower drawer
    B. *bad,* because the file cabinet may tip over when the top drawer is opened
    C. *good,* because it is the most easily reachable drawer for the average person
    D. *bad,* because a person bending down at another drawer may accidentally bang his head on the bottom of the drawer when he straightens up

32. If a senior typist or senior clerk has requisitioned a *ream* of paper in order to duplicate a single page office announcement, how many announcements can be printed from the one package of paper?

    A. 200　　B. 500　　C. 700　　D. 1,000

33. Your supervisor has asked you to locate a telephone number for an attorney named Jones, whose office is located at 311 Broadway, and whose name is not already listed in your files.
    The BEST method for finding the number would be for you to

    A. call the information operator and have her get it for you
    B. look in the alphabetical directory (white pages) under the name Jones at 311 Broadway
    C. refer to the heading Attorney in the yellow pages for the name Jones at 311 Broadway
    D. ask your supervisor who referred her to Mr. Jones, then call that person for the number

34. An example of material that should NOT be sent by first class mail is a

    A. email copy of a letter　　B. post card
    C. business reply card　　D. large catalogue

35. In the operations of a government agency, a voucher is ORDINARILY used to 35._____
    A. refer someone to the agency for a position or assignment
    B. certify that an agency's records of financial trans-actions are accurate
    C. order payment from agency funds of a stated amount to an individual
    D. enter a statement of official opinion in the records of the agency

Questions 36-40.

ENGLISH USAGE

DIRECTIONS: Each question from 36 through 40 contains a sentence. Read each sentence carefully to decide whether it is correct. Then, in the space at the right, mark your answer:

(A) if the sentence is incorrect because of bad grammar or sentence structure

(B) if the sentence is incorrect because of bad punctuation

(C) if the sentence is incorrect because of bad capitalization

(D) if the sentence is correct

Each incorrect sentence has only one type of error. Consider a sentence correct if it has no errors, although there may be other correct ways of saying the same thing.

SAMPLE QUESTION I: One of our clerks were promoted yesterday.

The subject of this sentence is *one,* so the verb should be *was promoted* instead of *were promoted.* Since the sentence is incorrect because of bad grammar, the answer to Sample Question I is (A).

SAMPLE QUESTION II: Between you and me, I would prefer not going there.

Since this sentence is correct, the answer to Sample Question II is (D).

36. The National alliance of Businessmen is trying to persuade private businesses to hire youth in the summertime. 36._____

37. The supervisor who is on vacation, is in charge of processing vouchers. 37._____

38. The activity of the committee at its conferences is always stimulating. 38._____

39. After checking the addresses again, the letters went to the mailroom. 39._____

40. The director, as well as the employees, are interested in sharing the dividends. 40._____

Questions 41-45.

FILING

DIRECTIONS: Each question from 41 through 45 contains four names. For each question, choose the name that should be FIRST if the four names are to be arranged in alphabeti-cal order in accordance with the Rules for Alphabetical Filing given below. Read these rules carefully. Then, for each question, indicate in the space at the right the letter before the name that should be FIRST in alphabet-ical order.

RULES FOR ALPHABETICAL FILING

Names of People

(1) The names of people are filed in strict alphabetical order, first according to the last name, then according to first name or initial, and finally according to middle name or initial. FOR EXAMPLE: George Allen comes before Edward Bell, and Leonard P. Reston comes before Lucille B. Reston.

(2) When last names are the same, FOR EXAMPLE, A. Green and Agnes Green, the one with the initial comes before the one with the name written out when the first initials are identi-cal.

(3) When first and last names are alike and the middle name is given, FOR EXAMPLE, John David Doe and John Devoe Doe, the names should be filed in the alphabetical order of the middle names.

(4) When first and last names are the same, a name without a middle initial comes before one with a middle name or initial. FOR EXAMPLE, John Doe comes before both John A. Doe and John Alan Doe.

(5) When first and last names are the same, a name with a middle initial comes before one with a middle name beginning with the same initial. FOR EXAMPLE: Jack R. Hertz comes before Jack Richard Hertz.

(6) Prefixes such as De, O', Mac, Mc, and Van are filed as written and are treated as part of the names to which they are connected. FOR EXAMPLE: Robert O'Dea is filed before David Olsen.

(7) Abbreviated names are treated as if they were spelled out. FOR EXAMPLE: Chas. is filed as Charles and Thos. is filed as Thomas.

(8) Titles and designations such as Dr., Mr., and Prof. are disregarded in filing.

Names of Organizations

(1) The names of business organizations are filed according to the order in which each word in the name appears. When an organization name bears the name of a person, it is filed according to the rules for filing names of people as given above. FOR EXAMPLE: William Smith Service Co. comes before Television Distributors, Inc.

(2) Where bureau, board, office, or department appears as the first part of the title of a governmental agency, that agency should be filed under the word in the title expressing the chief function of the agency. FOR EXAMPLE: Bureau of the Budget would be filed as if written Budget, (Bureau of the). The Department of Personnel would be filed as if written Personnel, (Department of).

(3) When the following words are part of an organization, they are disregarded: the, of, and.

(4) When there are numbers in a name, they are treated as if they were spelled out. FOR EXAMPLE: 10th Street Bootery is filed as Tenth Street Bootery.

SAMPLE QUESTION:
- A. Jane Earl (2)
- B. James A. Earle (4)
- C. James Earl (1)
- D. J. Earle (3)

The numbers in parentheses show the proper alphabetical order in which these names should be filed. Since the name that should be filed FIRST is James Earl, the answer to the Sample Question is (C).

41.
- A. Majorca Leather Goods
- B. Robert Maiorca and Sons
- C. Maintenance Management Corp.
- D. Majestic Carpet Mills

41.____

42.
- A. Municipal Telephone Service
- B. Municipal Reference Library
- C. Municipal Credit Union
- D. Municipal Broadcasting System

42.____

43.
- A. Robert B. Pierce
- B. R. Bruce Pierce
- C. Ronald Pierce
- D. Robert Bruce Pierce

43.____

44.
- A. Four Seasons Sports Club
- B. 14th. St. Shopping Center
- C. Forty Thieves Restaurant
- D. 42nd St. Theaters

44.____

45.
- A. Franco Franceschini
- B. Amos Franchini
- C. Sandra Franceschia
- D. Lilie Franchinesca

45.____

Questions 46-50.

SPELLING

DIRECTIONS: In each question, one of the words is misspelled. Select the letter of the misspelled word. *PRINT THE LETTER OF THE CORRECT ANSWER IN THE SPACE AT THE RIGHT.*

46.
- A. option
- B. extradite
- C. comparitive
- D. jealousy

46.____

47.
- A. handicaped
- B. assurance
- C. sympathy
- D. speech

47.____

48. A. recommend   B. carraige
    C. disapprove D. independent

49. A. ingenuity   B. tenet (opinion)
    C. uncanny   D. intrigueing

50. A. arduous   B. hideous
    C. iervant   D. companies

KEY (CORRECT ANSWERS)

1. A	11. D	21. A	31. B	41. C
2. B	12. B	22. D	32. B	42. D
3. D	13. D	23. C	33. C	43. B
4. B	14. B	24. A	34. D	44. D
5. D	15. A	25. C	35. C	45. C
6. C	16. B	26. D	36. C	46. C
7. A	17. C	27. D	37. B	47. A
8. C	18. D	28. B	38. D	48. B
9. D	19. A	29. A	39. A	49. D
10. B	20. C	30. C	40. A	50. C'

EXAMINATION SECTION

TEST 1

DIRECTIONS: Each question or incomplete statement is followed by several suggested answers or completions. Select the one that BEST answers the question or completes the statement. *PRINT THE LETTER OF THE CORRECT ANSWER IN THE SPACE AT THE RIGHT.*

1. Which of the following must be changed in order to implement a word processing system?
    A. Equipment
    B. Procedures
    C. Work relationships between people
    D. Methods of supervision
    E. All of the above

2. A type of word processing hardware/software configuration where several terminals share the same CPU is called a _____ configuration.
    A. shared logic
    B. single-user
    C. distributed logic
    D. multifunction
    E. timesharing

3. Current technology has led word processing hardware/software configurations toward
    A. centralized processing
    B. decentralized processing
    C. the use of mainframe computers
    D. the use of wide-area networks
    E. the increasing use of minicomputers over microcomputers to do word processing

4. A(n) _____ printer offers *letter quality* print.
    A. daisy wheel
    B. dot matrix
    C. laser
    D. ink jet
    E. all of the above

5. A _____ is an input device or software that can read handwritten or printed data, which may be later edited by a word processor.
    A. MICR
    B. OCR
    C. laser reader
    D. daisy wheel
    E. both A and B

6. A(n) _____ uses special software to do word processing functions.   6._____
   A. word processor   B. electronic typewriter
   C. computer processor   D. automatic typewriter
   E. electronic printer

7. Printed output is called   7._____
   A. soft copy   B. printout
   C. formatted output   D. hard copy
   E. none of the above

8. _____ transmits a word-processed document via electronic communications.   8._____
   A. TWX   B. Telecopy
   C. E-mail   D. Telex
   E. Modem

9. _____ refers to output on a video screen or computer monitor.   9._____
   A. Soft copy   B. Video copy
   C. Light output   D. Hard copy
   E. None of the above

10. _____ refers to output to microfilm instead of paper or video.   10._____
    A. TWX   B. Microfiche
    C. COM   D. Floppy disk output
    E. None of the above

11. A disadvantage of word processors is   11._____
    A. decreased effective typing speeds
    B. higher costs in producing documents
    C. that offices with word processors generate more paper than offices without word processors
    D. lower quality output than computer printers
    E. difficult revision of previously processed documents

12. Which of the following is a character that can be entered through a word processor?   12._____
    A. %   B. !
    C. [blank space]   D. +
    E. All of the above

13. A _____ can permanently store documents and files.   13._____
    A. printer   B. compact disc
    C. computer memory   D. CPU
    E. All of the above

14. Printers, disk drives, video screens and keyboards are examples of _____ equipment.
    A. output
    B. input
    C. processing
    D. peripheral
    E. storage

    14._____

15. A _____ features multi-color display.
    A. monochrome monitor
    B. plotter
    C. color monitor
    D. RGB output
    E. graphics monitor

    15._____

16. A(n) _____ printer forms characters by using a printhead to press pinpoints against a ribbon.
    A. laser
    B. ink jet
    C. daisy wheel
    D. dot matrix
    E. All of the above

    16._____

17. Which of the following is NOT an input device that may be used on a word processor?
    A. Mouse
    B. Keyboard
    C. Document scanner
    D. DVD
    E. All of the above

    17._____

18. The _____ is the position on the word processor screen that indicates where the next character will appear.
    A. pointer
    B. cell indicator
    C. status line
    D. cursor
    E. video pointer

    18._____

19. Which of the following functions allows the upward and downward movement of text lines on the screen?
    A. Cursor keys
    B. Scrolling
    C. Positioning
    D. Page breaking
    E. Blocking

    19._____

20. Which of the following functions allows text to be indicated for operations such as moving or copying?
    A. Cursor keys
    B. Scrolling
    C. Boilerplating
    D. Page breaking
    E. Blocking

    20._____

21. Which of the following types of word processing allows the operator to see on the screen *exactly* how the output will appear on paper? 21._____
    A. Text-formatted word processing
    B. WYSIWYG
    C. Off-screen formatting
    D. Typeset word processing
    E. Desktop publishing

22. Most word processors work with a screen length of _____ characters. 22._____
    A. 24   B. 50
    C. 65   D. 80
    E. None of the above

23. Most word processor screens will display _____ lines of text at a time. 23._____
    A. 80   B. 50
    C. 32   D. 24
    E. None of the above

24. Which of the following features is used to display information about a document being edited on the word processor, including the name of the document, line number and column number? 24._____
    A. ruler line   B. carriage bar
    C. status line   D. insert line
    E. tab set line

25. The _____ is used on the word processor screen to resemble the column and margin settings on a typewriter. 25._____
    A. ruler line   B. carriage bar
    C. status line   D. insert line
    E. tab set line

KEY (CORRECT ANSWERS)

1. E	11. C	21. B
2. A	12. E	22. D
3. B	13. B	23. D
4. E	14. D	24. C
5. B	15. C	25. A
6. A	16. D	
7. D	17. D	
8. C	18. D	
9. A	19. B	
10. C	20. E	

TEST 2

DIRECTIONS: Each question or incomplete statement is followed by several suggested answers or completions. Select the one that BEST answers the question or completes the statement. *PRINT THE LETTER OF THE CORRECT ANSWER IN THE SPACE AT THE RIGHT.*

1. Which of the following word-processing features enables the programmer to type characters continuously without pressing the carriage return at the end of the line?
   - A. Insert
   - B. Wraparound
   - C. Continuous type
   - D. Boilerplating
   - E. Reformatting

   1._____

2. A _____ carriage return is placed into a document by the word processor, not by the operator.
   - A. hard
   - B. soft
   - C. embedded
   - D. non-embedded
   - E. none of the above

   2._____

3. The spacing of words and letters within a line of type to make it meet both margins of a column is called
   - A. boilerplating
   - B. justification
   - C. margin alignment
   - D. microjustification
   - E. proportional spacing

   3._____

4. The spacing between characters and words on a line can be more evenly separated with
   - A. justification
   - B. boilerplating
   - C. microjustification
   - D. margin alignment
   - E. all of the above

   4._____

5. Commands placed into a document which affect the placement, shape and size of margins, headings, footings, and page numbers are called _____ commands.
   - A. on-screen format
   - B. embedded format
   - C. boilerplate embedded
   - D. dot
   - E. all of the above

   5._____

6. On a standard sheet of 11" x 8.5" paper, how many vertical lines are available for printing?
   - A. 6
   - B. 11
   - C. 50
   - D. 66
   - E. none of the above

   6._____

7. The study of the interaction between humans and machines is called
   A. ornithology
   B. metaphysics
   C. robotics
   D. ergonomics
   E. mechahumanism

   7._____

8. When the _____ key is held down, the character will be entered continuously until the key is released.
   A. alphabetic
   B. Dvorak
   C. numeric
   D. Qwerty
   E. auto-repeat

   8._____

9. This is a *toggle* key. When you press it, all alphabetic characters will be in uppercase. When you press it again, all alphabetic characters will be lowercase. This is the _____ key.
   A. numeric
   B. page down
   C. Alt
   D. caps lock
   E. return

   9._____

10. On most word-processing machines, the _____ keys execute a special function such as saving a document or centering a line of text.
    A. Esc
    B. Ctrl
    C. function
    D. Alt
    E. All of the above

    10._____

11. A _____ is an input device which can read data from printed or typed documents and enter it into the computer for further editing.
    A. scanner
    B. modem
    C. tracer
    D. TWX
    E. fax

    11._____

12. A printing term for fully formed characters is
    A. draft quality
    B. double strike
    C. letter quality
    D. dot matrix
    E. near letter quality

    12._____

13. _____ paper is used for printed output. It consists of individual sheets connected together, and perforated for easy detachment.
    A. single sheet
    B. fanfold
    C. continuous form
    D. Both A and B
    E. Both B and C

    13._____

14. The particular style and size in which a character may be printed is called
    A. typestyle
    B. font
    C. display
    D. pixel
    E. density

    14._____

15. Which of the following is an external storage media on which documents may be stored and retrieved from?
    A. Floppy disk
    B. Hard disk
    C. Compact disc
    D. External hard drive
    E. All of the above

15._____

16. Before a new floppy disk may be used on a specific word processor, it must be prepared for use with the word processor through a process called
    A. initializing
    B. formatting
    C. booting
    D. consolidation
    E. both B and C

16._____

17. A 10-megabyte hard disk can store the equivalent of _____ 360K floppy disks.
    A. 21
    B. 23
    C. 25
    D. 27
    E. 29

17._____

18. Generally speaking, how often should documents stored on computer disks be backed up for security and safety reasons?
    A. Annually
    B. Monthly
    C. Weekly
    D. Daily
    E. Multiple times daily

18._____

19. A method of document distribution in which a printed copy of the document may be sent over telephone lines is
    A. modemizing
    B. e-mail
    C. fax transmission
    D. digital transmission
    E. analog transmission

19._____

20. The _____ communicates between the word-processing hardware and software.
    A. operating system
    B. database system
    C. applications program
    D. command processor
    E. input/output manager

20._____

21. A listing of documents or files stored on a particular disk is called a
    A. catalog
    B. inventory
    C. directory
    D. data storage program
    E. menu

21._____

22. To facilitate the organization of documents on the disk, the _____ directory may be subdivided into other classifications of directories.
    A. root
    B. main
    D. sub
    D. path
    E. core

22._____

23. A _____ word-processing software help system displays help messages based upon the command being used at the moment. 23._____
   A. menu-driven
   B. context-sensitive
   C. command-driven
   D. reference-sensitive
   E. key-sensitive

24. A _____ word processor allows the user to choose an operation to be performed from a list of options. 24._____
   A. command-driven
   B. context-sensitive
   C. reference-sensitive
   D. menu-driven
   E. icon-driven

25. The _____ menu is usually used with a mouse. The menu descends from the top of the screen after it is pointed to by the mouse. 25._____
   A. pop-up
   B. sticky
   C. pull-down
   D. multi-level
   D. menu tree

KEY (CORRECT ANSWERS)

1. B	11. A	21. C
2. B	12. C	22. A
3. B	13. C	23. B
4. C	14. B	24. D
5. B	15. E	25. C
6. D	16. B	
7. D	17. D	
8. E	18. D	
9. D	19. C	
10. C	20. A	

EXAMINATION SECTION
TEST 1

DIRECTIONS: Each question or incomplete statement is followed by several suggested answers or completions. Select the one that BEST answers the question or completes the statement. *PRINT THE LETTER OF THE CORRECT ANSWER IN THE SPACE AT THE RIGHT.*

1. When a document has been previously saved on a disk, and the command is issued to save the document again, the

    A. document is erased from the disk
    B. document is stored in two different forms on the disk
    C. latest version of the document is saved and replaces the previous version
    D. document will not be saved
    E. document is erased from both the screen and disk

    1.____

2. If a previously saved document is being edited and the word processing operator does not want to save the new changes, the operator should

    A. turn off the machine
    B. save the document
    C. abandon the document without saving it
    D. rename the document
    E. reverse all previous editing changes one by one

    2.____

3. In a word-processed document, a period at the end of a sentence should be followed by_____ space(s).

    A. zero
    B. one
    C. two
    D. three
    E. one, two or three

    3.____

4. When a text is entered the_____ acts as a *signal* that the word processor automatically enters while wrapping words to the next line

    A. hard carriage return
    B. soft carriage return
    C. hard space
    D. soft space
    E. both A and C

    4.____

5. With_____ the word processing operator may move a document up and down, line by line on the screen.

    A. horizontal scrolling
    B. vertical scrolling
    C. paging
    D. diagonal scrolling
    E. none of the above

    5.____

6. On the word processor, the_____ mode overwrites any previously typed text.

    A. insert
    B. overwrite
    C. strikeover
    D. delete
    E. all of the above

    6.____

7. Two hyphenated words connected by the_____ will not split at the right margin and will always appear on the same line.

   A. soft hyphen
   B. hard hyphen
   C. soft carriage return
   D. hard carriage return
   E. hard space

8. The realignment of text after editing so that it is aligned with the margins is called

   A. paragraph reform
   B. pagination
   C. repagination
   D. blocking
   E. re-editing

9. A function used to calculate or recalculate page breaks on a document is called

   A. repagination
   B. paragraph reform
   C. document reform
   D. blocking
   E. paging

10. The process of moving and copying a block of text from one place to another is called

    A. blocking
    B. moving
    C. copying
    D. cutting and pasting
    E. all of the above

11. A string of characters may consist of which kinds of characters?

    A. Numbers
    B. Letters
    C. Special characters (*,!,&, etc.)
    D. Phrases
    E. All of the above

12. A *search and replace* option which finds all occurrences of a search item and automatically replaces it is called_____ search and replace.

    A. item
    B. case-sensitive
    C. automatic
    D. wildcard
    E. global

13. Assume you wish to search for the word "row." You specify that the search NOT be case sensitive. In which of the following phrases would the word be found?

    A. Rowboat
    B. Front Row Seats
    C. Arrow
    D. Row, row, row your boat
    E. All of the above

14. A program used by the word-processing software to find a synonym for a certain word in a document is a(n)

    A. algorithm
    B. spell checker
    C. style and grammar checker
    D. thesaurus
    E. all of the above

15. The settings initially entered into word processing software by its designers indicate initial settings, such as the right and left margins, or perhaps the number of lines per page. These settings can usually be changed by the user.
    This refers to

    A. default settings
    B. configuration settings
    C. set-up file
    D. initialization settings
    E. format settings

16. A single line ending a paragraph that appears by itself at the top of a page is called a(n)

    A. widow
    B. orphan
    C. single line paragraph
    D. soft page break
    E. hard page break

17. The first line of a paragraph that appears by itself as the last line of a page is called a(n)

    A. widow
    B. orphan
    C. single line paragraph
    D. soft page break
    E. hard page break

18. A specific code in one page of a document refers to a page or other number elsewhere in the document. The code always correctly displays the number to which it refers even if that number is changed.
    This paragraph describes the feature known as

    A. automatic page breaking
    B. hard page breaking
    C. symbolic referencing
    D. repagination
    E. formatting

19. _____ allows entire pages of text to be centered in the middle of the page.

    A. Horizontal alignment
    B. Centering
    C. Vertical alignment
    D. Justification
    E. Blocking

20. _____ refers to the number of characters printed per inch.

    A. Pica
    B. Elite
    C. Microjustification
    D. Helvetica
    E. Pitch

21. Which of the following is NOT a typeface?

    A. Elite
    B. Pica
    C. Times Roman
    D. Helvetica
    E. Hearst

22. Of the following, which is the SMALLEST type size?

    A. 8 pitch
    B. 8 point
    C. 10 point
    D. 10 pitch
    E. 14 point

23. A certain method assigns more or less space to characters based upon their width. For example, the letter "i" is given less space than the letter "m" when printed.
    This refers to

    A. fixed spacing
    B. fixed pitch
    C. proportional spacing
    D. microjustification
    E. justification

24. The _____ comes on a floppy or hard disk. It is loaded into the memory of the word processor, and is used when needed.

    A. internal font
    B. cartridge font
    C. font server
    D. memory font
    E. downloadable font

25. Columns of numbers which may include decimal points are aligned with 25.____

    A. justification
    B. horizontal tabs
    C. decimal tabs
    D. tab stops
    E. tab columns

KEY (CORRECT ANSWERS)

1.	C	11.	E
2.	C	12.	E
3.	C	13.	E
4.	B	14.	D
5.	A	15.	A
6.	C	16.	A
7.	B	17.	B
8.	A	18.	C
9.	A	19.	C
10.	D	20.	E

21. E
22. B
23. C
24. E
25. C

TEST 2

DIRECTIONS: Each question or incomplete statement is followed by several suggested answers or completions. Select the one that BEST answers the question or completes the statement. *PRINT THE LETTER OF THE CORRECT ANSWER IN THE SPACE AT THE RIGHT.*

1. Examine the following paragraph:
   Working with a word processor allows a person to be more productive than when working with a typewriter.
   This type of indentation is called a(n):

   A. hanging indent
   B. reverse indent
   C. outdent
   D. all of the above
   E. none of the above

   1.____

2. Which of the following contains a superscript?

   A. Copyright©
   B. 70°
   C. H_2O
   D. word
   E. none of the above

   2.____

3. While a document is being printed, the word processing operator may wish to *set up* other documents so that they may begin being printed when a previous document has finished printing. To accomplish this, the operator may use a

   A. spooler
   B. print queue
   C. line transmitter
   D. batch file
   E. delay tray

   3.____

4. Printing a document along the wide axis of the page, as shown below, is called_____mode.

   A. landscape
   B. portrait
   C. lengthwise
   D. widthwise
   E. axis

   4.____

5. When creating a merged document in order to print form letters, the document which contains the unchanging parts of the letter is called the

   A. variable document
   B. boilerplate
   C. secondary file
   D. primary document
   E. all of the above

   5.____

6. With secondary files to be merged into a file, each individual item that makes up a record in the secondary file is called a

   A. file
   B. character
   C. item
   D. record
   E. database

   6.____

7. Arranging data in order by last name and code number is called

   A. arranging
   B. indexing
   C. sorting
   D. placement
   E. relative positioning

   7.____

8. The word processor uses the _____ code to represent special characters, regular characters, and numbers.

   A. binary
   B. hexadecimal
   C. octal
   D. ASCII
   E. OCR

9. The type of columnar output seen in newspaper, newsletter, or magazine output is called

   A. snaking columns
   B. newsletter columns
   C. magazine columns
   D. flowing columns
   E. bulleting

10. _____ is where white characters are printed against a black background.

    A. Kerning
    B. Dropout type
    C. Leading
    D. Reverse video
    E. Inverse video

11. When using a word processor to do desktop publishing, the type of video monitor that is MOST desirable is the

    A. high resolution monochrome
    B. color with VGA
    C. color with EGA
    D. color with UGA
    E. low resolution monochrome

12. A divided or sectioned video screen that allows you to look at two or more parts of the same document or two different documents at once is the

    A. vertical loop
    B. window
    C. submenu
    D. alternate view file
    E. kern

13. A recording of a set of keystrokes repeatedly played over and over again with just the touch of one or a few keystrokes is described as

    A. kerning
    B. leading
    C. macro
    D. program
    E. stored instructions

14. On word processors which can perform arithmetic operations, which key would be used to perform multiplication?

    A. x
    B. X
    C. *
    D. ^
    E. /

15. If performing an arithmetic function with a word processor, the outcome of the following function - (100 + 200 x 5) - would be

    A. 305
    B. 1,500
    C. 500
    D. 1,100
    E. none of the above

16. If a word processor wished to send a document to a remote word processor via telephone lines, the operator would use _____ to transmit the document.

    A. TWX
    B. modem
    C. modulator
    D. demodulator
    E. CCD

17. If a *write protect tab* is affixed to the write protect notch on a disk,

    A. both reading and writing can take place on the disk
    B. only reading may take place from the disk
    C. only writing may take place to the disk
    D. neither reading or writing may take place
    E. only previously stored documents may be read from and written to the disk

18. A _____ is used in a search, or search and replace option, to represent characters in the same position in the string being searched for

    A. delimiter
    B. wild card
    C. replace character
    D. op character
    E. search string

19. The most important advantage of using a word processor instead of a typewriter is the ability to

    A. print documents at high speed
    B. easily revise and edit documents
    C. store large amounts of data on computer disk
    D. automatically check documents for spelling
    E. print multiple copies of a single document

20. The greatest benefit derived by a company that uses word processing is

    A. cost savings
    B. greater employee productivity and efficiency
    C. better looking documents
    D. a "paperless" office
    E. all of the above

21. _____ paper allows for carbonless copies.

    A. Carbon
    B. Continuous form
    C. Impact
    D. Action
    E. Bursting

22. The _____ is NOT a word processor peripheral device.

    A. printer
    B. diskdrive
    C. video display
    D. keyboard
    E. memory

23. Documents that are to be bound usually must have a larger margin on the left-hand side to accommodate binding.
    This distance is measured by

    A. page offset
    B. left margin offset
    C. left justification
    D. microjustification
    E. binding margin

24. Some word processors allow the documents to be integrated with other computer software packages. One type of computer software package that arranges numbers in columns and rows for arithmetic analysis is called a(n)

   A. database management system
   B. utility program
   C. records management system
   D. calculator program
   E. electronic spreadsheet

25. Assume that the asterisk (*) is a *wild card* character for performing a search function on the word processor. If we wanted to search for the text entitled "National Learning Corporation," or any part thereof, a valid search string would be

   A. National * Corporation
   B. National Learning * Corporation
   C. ******** Learning Corporation
   D. ******** LEARNING CORPORATION
   E. they are all valid

KEY (CORRECT ANSWERS)

1. D	11. A
2. B	12. B
3. B	13. C
4. A	14. C
5. B	15. D
6. D	16. B
7. C	17. B
8. D	18. B
9. A	19. B
10. B	20. B

21. D
22. E
23. A
24. E
25. C

TESTS IN SPELLING

EXAMINATION SECTION
TEST 1

DIRECTIONS: In each question of the following tests, select the letter of the one MISSPELLED word in each of the listed groups of five (5) words. *PRINT THE LETTER OF THE CORRECT ANSWER IN THE SPACE AT THE RIGHT.*

1.	A.	break	B.	scenary	C.	business	D.	arouse	E.	religious	1.____
2.	A.	rinsed	B.	height	C.	jewel	D.	furtile	E.	doesn't	2.____
3.	A.	perform	B.	divide	C.	apologize	D.	occasion	E.	acheive	3.____
4.	A.	asending	B.	benefit	C.	disappear	D.	operate	E.	grammar	4.____
5.	A.	forty	B.	precede	C.	annuel	D.	parable	E.	curiosity	5.____
6.	A.	irritable	B.	stupefy	C.	gaseous	D.	millionair	E.	luscious	6.____
7.	A.	invincible	B.	Slav	C.	supersede	D.	haddock	E.	fatigueing	7.____
8.	A.	scissors	B.	explanatory	C.	bituminus	D.	heifer	E.	cessation	8.____
9.	A.	caramel	B.	Wisconsin	C.	acquarium	D.	sterilize	E.	pseudonym	9.____
10.	A.	precipise	B.	knapsack	C.	brilliance	D.	challenge	E.	decrepit	10.____
11.	A.	certificate	B.	ajourn	C.	apparel	D.	aggression	E.	symphony	11.____
12.	A.	Norwegian	B.	constent	C.	interruption	D.	wouldn't	E.	article	12.____
13.	A.	heros	B.	logical	C.	guarantee	D.	imprison	E.	legitimate	13.____
14.	A.	happiness	B.	weird	C.	miscellaneous	D.	village	E.	arguement	14.____
15.	A.	wretched	B.	tendency	C.	controversiel	D.	arbitrary	E.	denial	15.____
16.	A.	lonliness	B.	safeguard	C.	pilot	D.	chiefs	E.	obstacle	16.____
17.	A.	shining	B.	professional	C.	scheme	D.	excitment	E.	expectancy	17.____
18.	A.	negative	B.	editorial	C.	clothe	D.	economize	E.	suprising	18.____
19.	A.	illegal	B.	opinion	C.	discription	D.	rationalize	E.	picnicking	19.____
20.	A.	circuit	B.	sponser	C.	exasperate	D.	volume	E.	valuable	20.____

KEY (CORRECT ANSWERS)

1. B. scenery
2. D. fertile
3. E. achieve
4. A. ascending
5. C. annual
6. D. millionaire
7. E. fatiguing
8. C. bituminous
9. C. aquarium
10. A. precipice
11. B. adjourn
12. B. constant
13. A. heroes
14. E. argument
15. C. controversial
16. A. loneliness
17. D. excitement
18. E. surprising
19. C. description
20. B. sponsor

TEST 2

DIRECTIONS: In each question of the following tests, select the letter of the one MISSPELLED word in each of the listed groups of five (5) words. *PRINT THE LETTER OF THE CORRECT ANSWER IN THE SPACE AT THE RIGHT.*

1. A. procession B. performance C. poize D. allied E. discipline 1.____
2. A. advocate B. saleries C. commercial D. expense E. forcibly 2.____
3. A. enormous B. enterprise C. florist D. humilliate E. careful 3.____
4. A. treachery B. bolstor C. simplify D. revelation E. reciprocal 4.____
5. A. witness B. derisive C. typewriter D. relative E. medecine 5.____
6. A. betrayel B. forsaken C. impetuous D. finesse E. recognize 6.____
7. A. forcast B. pastime C. several D. ridiculous E. cleanliness 7.____
8. A. correspond B. conceited C. implies D. receptacle E. amatuer 8.____
9. A. captain B. definitely C. credited D. cordially E. couragous 9.____
10. A. parallel B. various C. obnoxious D. assurence E. grateful 10.____
11. A. feirce B. ascent C. allies D. doctor E. coming 11.____
12. A. hopeless B. absense C. foretell D. certain E. similar 12.____
13. A. advise B. muscle C. manual D. provocation E. copywright 13.____
14. A. behooves B. reservoir C. frostbiten D. squalor E. ambuscade 14.____
15. A. systematic B. precious C. tremenduous D. insulation E. brilliant 15.____
16. A. significant B. jurisdiction C. libel D. monkies E. legacy 16.____
17. A. delicatessen B. occupansy C. gorgeous D. consolation E. anxiety 17.____
18. A. tyranny B. perennial C. catagory D. inspector E. confidential 18.____
19. A. symbol B. formerly C. warring D. caution E. bankrupcy 19.____
20. A. aperture B. cellaphane C. diagnosis D. intestinal E. mahogany 20.____

KEY (CORRECT ANSWERS)

1. C. poise
2. B. salaries
3. D. humiliate
4. B. bolster
5. E. medicine
6. A. betrayal
7. A. forecast
8. E. amateur
9. E. courageous
10. D. assurance
11. A. fierce
12. B. abscence
13. E. copyright
14. C. frostbitten
15. C. tremendous
16. D. monkeys
17. B. occupancy
18. C. category
19. E. bankruptcy
20. B. cellophane

TEST 3

DIRECTIONS: In each question of the following tests, select the letter of the one MISSPELLED word in each of the listed groups of five (5) words. *PRINT THE LETTER OF THE CORRECT ANSWER IN THE SPACE AT THE RIGHT.*

1. A. pitiful B. latter C. ommitted D. agreement E. reconcile 1.____
2. A. banaana B. routine C. likewise D. indecent E. habitually 2.____
3. A. relieve B. copys C. ninety D. crowded E. electoral 3.____
4. A. adviseable B. illustrative C. financial D. nevertheless E. chimneys 4.____
5. A. prisioner B. immediate C. statistics D. surgeon E. treachery 5.____
6. A. option B. extradite C. comparitive D. jealousy E. illusion 6.____
7. A. handicaped B. assurance C. sympathy D. speech E. dining 7.____
8. A. recommend B. carraige C. disapprove D. independent E. mortgage 8.____
9. A. systematic B. ingenuity C. tenet D. uncanny E. intrigueing 9.____
10. A. arduous B. hideous C. fervant D. companies E. breach 10.____
11. A. together B. attempt C. loyality D. innocent E. rinse 11.____
12. A. argueing B. emergency C. kindergarten D. religious E. schedule 12.____
13. A. society B. anticipate C. dissatisfy D. responsable E. temporary 13.____
14. A. chaufeur B. grammar C. planned D. dining room E. accurate 14.____
15. A. confidence B. maturity C. aspiration D. evasion E. insurence 15.____
16. A. unnecessary B. dirigible C. transparant D. similar E. appetite 16.____
17. A. regional B. slimy C. tumbler D. educator E. femenine 17.____
18. A. orchestration B. proclamation C. pretext D. rearmement E. invoice 18.____
19. A. fragrant B. independent C. halves D. parallel E. advantagous 19.____
20. A. championing B. conversion C. predominent D. puppet E. anarchist 20.____

KEY (CORRECT ANSWERS)

1. C. omitted
2. A. banana
3. B. copies
4. A. advisable
5. A. prisoner
6. C. comparative
7. A. handicapped
8. B. carriage
9. E. intriguing
10. C. fervent
11. C. loyalty
12. A. arguing
13. D. responsible
14. A. chauffeur
15. E. insurance
16. C. transparent
17. E. feminine
18. D. rearmament
19. E. advantageous
20. C. predominant

TEST 4

DIRECTIONS: In each question of the following tests, select the letter of the one MIS-SPELLED word in each of the listed groups of five (5) words. *PRINT THE LETTER OF THE CORRECT ANSWER IN THE SPACE AT THE RIGHT.*

1. A. wrist B. welfare C. necessity D. scenery E. tendancy 1.____
2. A. commiting B. accusation C. endurance D. agreeable E. excitable 2.____
3. A. despair B. surgury C. privilege D. appreciation E. journeying 3.____
4. A. cameos B. propaganda C. delicious D. heathen E. interupt 4.____
5. A. relieve B. disappear C. development D. matress E. ninety-nine 5.____
6. A. finally B. bulitin C. doctor D. desirable E. sincerely 6.____
7. A. wrest B. array C. auspices D. sacrafice E. generations 7.____
8. A. liquid B. vegetable C. silence D. familiar E. fasinate 8.____
9. A. tomato B. suspence C. leisure D. license E. permanent 9.____
10. A. characteristic B. soliciting C. repititious D. immediately E. extravagant 10.____
11. A. travel B. conductor C. equiping D. proposal E. twofold 11.____
12. A. philosopher B. minority C. managment D. emergency E. bibliography 12.____
13. A. constructive B. employee C. stalwart D. masterpeice E. theoretical 13.____
14. A. dissappoint B. volcanic C. illiterate D. myth E. superficial 14.____
15. A. totally B. penninsula C. sandwich D. ripening E. salvation 15.____
16. A. pastel B. aisle C. primarly D. journalistic E. diminished 16.____
17. A. warrier B. unification C. enamel D. defendant E. sustained 17.____
18. A. incidental B. lubricent C. conversion D. jurisdiction E. interpretation 18.____
19. A. auxilary B. boundaries C. session D. fabric E. ceiling 19.____
20. A. imperious B. depreciate C. rebutal D. wharf E. giddy 20.____

KEY (CORRECT ANSWERS)

1. E. tendency
2. A. committing
3. B. surgery
4. E. interrupt
5. D. mattress
6. B. bulletin
7. D. sacrifice
8. E. fascinate
9. B. suspense
10. C. repetitious
11. C. equipping
12. C. management
13. D. masterpiece
14. A. disappoint
15. B. peninsula
16. C. primarily
17. A. warrior
18. B. lubricant
19. A. auxiliary
20. C. rebuttal

TEST 5

DIRECTIONS: In each question of the following tests, select the letter of the one MISSPELLED word in each of the listed groups of five (5) words. *PRINT THE LETTER OF THE CORRECT ANSWER IN THE SPACE AT THE RIGHT.*

1. A. renewel   B. charitable   C. abrupt   D. humankind   E. strengthen   1.____
2. A. khaki   B. survival   C. laboratory   D. intensefied   E. stature   2.____
3. A. diesel   B. cocoa   C. alphabettical   D. visible   E. overlaid   3.____
4. A. neutral   B. ballot   C. parallysis   D. enterprise   E. abnormal   4.____
5. A. ironical   B. mountainous   C. permissible   D. carburetor   E. blizard   5.____
6. A. penalty   B. affidavit   C. document   D. notery   E. valid   6.____
7. A. provocative   B. apparition   C. forfiet   D. procedure   E. requisite   7.____
8. A. terrifying   B. museum   C. minimum   D. competitors   E. efficiensy   8.____
9. A. hangar   B. spokesman   C. mustache   D. cathederal   E. pumpkin   9.____
10. A. guidance   B. until   C. usage   D. loyalist   E. prarie   10.____
11. A. obnoxious   B. balancing   C. squadron   D. illicit   E. clearence   11.____
12. A. timetable   B. gymnasium   C. humid   D. disolve   E. gracious   12.____
13. A. spiciness   B. bibliography   C. injunction   D. mediator   E. discriminate   13.____
14. A. endearing   B. mannerism   C. predecesser   D. gardener   E. instantaneous   14.____
15. A. shrewdness   B. purified   C. acceptable   D. uniqueness   E. corugated   15.____
16. A. baptize   B. diversity   C. parochial   D. abandonning   E. hypnosis   16.____
17. A. deteryorate   B. priority   C. cuddle   D. shrivel   E. narcotic   17.____
18. A. neutrality   B. horseradish   C. contemporaries   D. inducement   E. prelimnery   18.____
19. A. eventually   B. disilusioned   C. divine   D. inimitable   E. fraudulent   19.____
20. A. verticle   B. musician   C. tomatoes   D. athletic   E. decision   20.____

KEY (CORRECT ANSWERS)

1. A. renewal
2. D. intensified
3. C. alphabetical
4. C. paralysis
5. E. blizzard
6. D. notary
7. C. forfeit
8. E. efficiency
9. D. cathedral
10. E. prairie
11. E. clearance
12. D. dissolve
13. B. bibliography
14. C. predecessor
15. E. corrugated
16. D. abandoning
17. A. deteriorate
18. E. preliminary
19. B. disillusioned
20. A. vertical

TEST 6

DIRECTIONS: In each question of the following tests, select the letter of the one MISSPELLED word in each of the listed groups of five (5) words. *PRINT THE LETTER OF THE CORRECT ANSWER IN THE SPACE AT THE RIGHT.*

1.	A.	advising	B.	recognize	C.	seize	D.	supply	E.	tradegy	1.____
2.	A.	intensive	B.	stationary	C.	benifit	D.	equipped	E.	preferring	2.____
3.	A.	predjudice	B.	pervade	C.	excel	D.	capitol	E.	chimneys	3.____
4.	A.	all right	B.	ninty	C.	cronies	D.	nervous	E.	separate	4.____
5.	A.	atheletic	B.	queue	C.	furl	D.	schedule	E.	abusing	5.____
6.	A.	skein	B.	wholesome	C.	witches	D.	coherent	E.	defenite	6.____
7.	A.	aggravate	B.	counsel	C.	deplorable	D.	proficency	E.	catarrh	7.____
8.	A.	suppressed	B.	lugubrious	C.	pecuniary	D.	boulevard	E.	fourty-fourth	8.____
9.	A.	militarism	B.	pilot	C.	crimnal	D.	monotonous	E.	tendency	9.____
10.	A.	prevalent	B.	berth	C.	auxiliary	D.	priveleges	E.	women's	10.____
11.	A.	incurred	B.	cieling	C.	strengthen	D.	carnage	E.	typical	11.____
12.	A.	twins	B.	year's	C.	acutely	D.	changible	E.	facility	12.____
13.	A.	deliscious	B.	enormous	C.	likeness	D.	witnesses	E.	commodity	13.____
14.	A.	scenes	B.	enlargement	C.	discretion	D.	acknowledging	E.	sesion	14.____
15.	A.	annum	B.	strenuous	C.	tretchery	D.	infamy	E.	opportune	15.____
16.	A.	marmelade	B.	loot	C.	kinsman	D.	crochet	E.	hawser	16.____
17.	A.	fireman	B.	glossary	C.	tuition	D.	dissapoint	E.	refrigerator	17.____
18.	A.	inadequate	B.	municpal	C.	bored	D.	masonic	E.	utilize	18.____
19.	A.	partisan	B.	temporary	C.	cawleflower	D.	obstinacy	E.	hyperbole	19.____
20.	A.	people's	B.	spherical	C.	foliage	D.	everlasting	E.	feesable	20.____

KEY (CORRECT ANSWERS)

1. E. tragedy
2. C. benefit
3. A. prejudice
4. B. ninety
5. A. athletic
6. E. definite
7. D. proficiency
8. E. forty-fourth
9. C. criminal
10. D. privileges
11. B. ceiling
12. D. changeable
13. A. delicious
14. E. session
15. C. treachery
16. A. marmalade
17. D. disappoint
18. B. municipal
19. C. cauliflower
20. E. feasible

TEST 7

DIRECTIONS: In each question of the following tests, select the letter of the one MISSPELLED word in each of the listed groups of five (5) words. *PRINT THE LETTER OF THE CORRECT ANSWER IN THE SPACE AT THE RIGHT.*

1. A. inferred   B. whisle   C. jovial   D. conscript   E. gracious   1.____
2. A. tantalizing   B. ominous   C. conductor   D. duchess   E. telagram   2.____
3. A. reconcile   B. primitive   C. sausy   D. quinine   E. cede   3.____
4. A. immagine   B. viaduct   C. chisel   D. Saturn   E. currant   4.____
5. A. amplify   B. greace   C. cholera   D. perilous   E. theology   5.____
6. A. pursevere   B. deodorize   C. ligament   D. illuminate   E. dropsy   6.____
7. A. legible   B. frivolously   C. precious   D. rezemblence   E. congeal   7.____
8. A. intramural   B. epidemic   C. germicide   D. anonymous   E. acurracy   8.____
9. A. affable   B. hazard   C. combustable   D. lacquer   E. stationary   9.____
10. A. sagacious   B. interpreter   C. poultise   D. dinosaur   E. dismal   10.____
11. A. acknowledging   B. deligate   C. foliage   D. staid   E. loot   11.____
12. A. gardian   B. losing   C. notwithstanding   D. worlds   E. typhoid   12.____
13. A. medal   B. utilize   C. efficiency   D. apricot   E. soliceting   13.____
14. A. museum   B. Christian   C. possesion   D. occasional   E. bored   14.____
15. A. capitol   B. sieze   C. premises   D. fragrance   E. tonnage   15.____
16. A. requisition   B. faculties   C. canon   D. chaufur   E. stomach   16.____
17. A. solemn   B. ascertain   C. I'll   D. chef   E. delinquant   17.____
18. A. parliments   B. distributor   C. voluntary   D. lovable   E. counsel   18.____
19. A. morale   B. democrat   C. rhumatism   D. dormitory   E. leased   19.____
20. A. screech   B. missapropriating   C. courtesies   D. wretched   E. furlough   20.____

KEY (CORRECT ANSWERS)

1. B. whistle
2. E. telegram
3. C. saucy
4. A. imagine
5. B. grease
6. A. persevere
7. D. resemblance
8. E. accuracy
9. C. combustible
10. C. poultice
11. B. delegate
12. A. guardian
13. E. soliciting
14. C. possession
15. B. seize
16. D. chauffeur
17. E. delinquent
18. A. parliaments
19. C. rheumatism
20. B. misappropriating

TEST 8

DIRECTIONS: In each question of the following tests, select the letter of the one MISSPELLED word in each of the listed groups of five (5) words. *PRINT THE LETTER OF THE CORRECT ANSWER IN THE SPACE AT THE RIGHT.*

1.	A.	typhoid	B.	tarriff	C.	visible	D.	accent	E.	countries	1.___
2.	A.	dizzy	B.	leggings	C.	steak	D.	compaine	E.	interior	2.___
3.	A.	profit	B.	tiranny	C.	shocked	D.	response	E.	innocent	3.___
4.	A.	freshman	B.	vague	C.	larsiny	D.	ignorant	E.	worrying	4.___
5.	A.	disatesfied	B.	jealous	C.	unfortunately	D.	economical	E.	lettuce	5.___
6.	A.	based	B.	primarily	C.	condemned	D.	accompanied	E.	dupped	6.___
7.	A.	superntendant	B.	veil	C.	congenial	D.	quantities	E.	ere	7.___
8.	A.	unanimous	B.	dessert	C.	undoubtedly	D.	kolera	E.	nuisance	8.___
9.	A.	woman's	B.	bulletin	C.	'tis	D.	Pullman	E.	envellop	9.___
10.	A.	initiate	B.	guardian	C.	pagent	D.	wretched	E.	adieu	10.___
11.	A.	continually	B.	guild	C.	vegtable	D.	vague	E.	patience	11.___
12.	A.	desease	B.	parole	C.	gallery	D.	awkward	E.	you'd	12.___
13.	A.	border	B.	warrant	C.	operated	D.	economics	E.	ilegal	13.___
14.	A.	fatal	B.	agatation	C.	obliged	D.	studying	E.	resignation	14.___
15.	A.	ammendment	B.	promptness	C.	glimpse	D.	canon	E.	tract	15.___
16.	A.	wholly	B.	apricot	C.	destruction	D.	pappal	E.	leisure	16.___
17.	A.	issuing	B.	rabbid	C.	unauthorized	D.	parasite	E.	khaki	17.___
18.	A.	nowadays	B.	courtesies	C.	negotiate	D.	gaurdian	E.	derrick	18.___
19.	A.	partisan	B.	seanse	C.	vacancy	D.	fragrance	E.	corps	19.___
20.	A.	equipped	B.	nuisance	C.	phrenoligist	D.	foreign	E.	insignia	20.___

KEY (CORRECT ANSWERS)

1. B. tariff
2. D. company
3. B. tyranny
4. C. larceny
5. A. dissatisfied
6. E. duped
7. A. superintendent
8. D. cholera
9. E. envelope
10. C. pageant
11. C. vegetable
12. A. disease
13. E. illegal
14. B. agitation
15. A. amendment
16. D. papal
17. B. rabid
18. D. guardian
19. B. seance
20. C. phrenologist

TEST 9

DIRECTIONS: In each question of the following tests, select the letter of the one MIS-SPELLED word in each of the listed groups of five (5) words. *PRINT THE LETTER OF THE CORRECT ANSWER IN THE SPACE AT THE RIGHT.*

1. A. frightfully   B. mantain   C. post office   D. specific   E. bachelor   1.____
2. A. cease   B. turkeys   C. woman's   D. hustling   E. weild   2.____
3. A. expedition   B. valuoble   C. typhoid   D. grapevines   E. advice   3.____
4. A. echoes   B. absolutly   C. foggy   D. wretched   E. Sabbath   4.____
5. A. screech   B. motorist   C. congresionel   D. utilize   E. eligible   5.____
6. A. quizzes   B. coarse   C. aquaintence   D. exhibition   E. totally   6.____
7. A. principle   B. transferring   C. statutes   D. here's   E. sergeon   7.____
8. A. porcilane   B. primeval   C. suite   D. unauthorized   E. declension   8.____
9. A. commodity   B. mischevious   C. galvanized   D. ordinance   E. tuition   9.____
10. A. Christian   B. fraternity   C. accompanying   D. disernable   E. inadequate   10.____
11. A. subsidy   B. inference   C. chronicle   D. purchace   E. adroit   11.____
12. A. resources   B. cargoes   C. oponent   D. disbelief   E. treasurer   12.____
13. A. origional   B. provincial   C. knuckle   D. ridiculous   E. ecstasy   13.____
14. A. attitude   B. soloes   C. occurred   D. policies   E. technique   14.____
15. A. opinionated B. quantity   C. systematic   D. drought   E. confidencial 15.____
16. A. interim   B. idleness   C. accesion   D. elite   E. fungi   16.____
17. A. inarticulate B. servitude   C. ejaculate   D. herewith   E. preceedence   17.____
18. A. experimental B. minority   C. cultural   D. expedient   E. penant   18.____
19. A. apparently   B. criticism   C. justification   D. physican   E. simultaneous 19.____
20. A. accidentally B. overule   C. unintentional   D. talented   E. maturation   20.____

111

KEY (CORRECT ANSWERS)

1. B. maintain
2. E. wield
3. B. valuable
4. B. absolutely
5. C. congressional
6. C. acquaintance
7. E. surgeon
8. A. porcelain
9. B. mischievous
10. D. discernible
11. D. purchase
12. C. opponent
13. A. original
14. B. solos
15. E. confidential
16. C. accession
17. E. precedence
18. E. pennant
19. D. physician
20. B. overrule

TEST 10

DIRECTIONS: In each question of the following tests, select the letter of the one MISSPELLED word in each of the listed groups of five (5) words. *PRINT THE LETTER OF THE CORRECT ANSWER IN THE SPACE AT THE RIGHT.*

1. A. liabillity B. capacity C. guidance D. illegible E. expedient 1.____
2. A. debris B. apetite C. mosquitoes D. vessal E. yacht 2.____
3. A. tireless B. feindish C. recruit D. swarthy E. sandal 3.____
4. A. redouble B. wizard C. murdurer D. hindrance E. syncope 4.____
5. A. equalize B. turbulent C. repetitive D. corronation E. statistical 5.____
6. A. remittance B. sensitivity C. fatality D. soprano E. inconveniance 6.____
7. A. fraternity B. plebeian C. inteligible D. trickster E. expeditionary 7.____
8. A. gasous B. consistency C. brooches D. magistrate E. translucent 8.____
9. A. lightning B. persistent C. cynical D. musician E. recipricate 9.____
10. A. commodity B. fictitous C. rabid D. gaiety E. couldn't 10.____
11. A. visible B. creditor C. paradice D. infinite E. questionnaire 11.____
12. A. existence B. disarming C. endorsement D. commercal E. trigger 12.____
13. A. aluminum B. stuning C. allowance D. irate E. pleasantry 13.____
14. A. cipher B. colloquial C. envoy D. pursued E. writting 14.____
15. A. insurable B. benign C. influential D. sophomore E. casualty 15.____
16. A. presentiment B. theological C. anatamy D. eccentricity E. amphibious 16.____
17. A. embargo B. vocalize C. recommend D. confering E. remunerate 17.____
18. A. tangent B. fickel C. circuit D. mathematics E. vegetarian 18.____
19. A. unscheduled B. declension C. secretariat D. forsight E. enamel 19.____
20. A. hygienic B. arrogant C. disbanded D. census E. memorandem 20.____

KEY (CORRECT ANSWERS)

1. A. liability
2. B. appetite
3. B. fiendish
4. C. murderer
5. D. coronation
6. E. inconvenience
7. C. intelligible
8. A. gaseous
9. E. reciprocate
10. B. fictitious
11. C. paradise
12. D. commercial
13. B. stunning
14. E. writing
15. C. influential
16. C. anatomy
17. D. conferring
18. B. fickle
19. D. foresight
20. E. memorandum

TESTS IN SPELLING

EXAMINATION SECTION
TEST 1

DIRECTIONS: In each question of the following tests, select the letter of the one MISSPELLED word in each of the listed groups of five (5) words. *PRINT THE LETTER OF THE CORRECT ANSWER IN THE SPACE AT THE RIGHT.*

1. A. barely B. assigned C. mechanical D. concequently E. lovingly 1._____
2. A. obedient B. elaborate C. disgust D. bearing E. ambasador 2._____
3. A. awkward B. charitable C. typhoid D. compitition E. ruffle 3._____
4. A. concervatory B. ninth C. morsel D. squirrels E. luxury 4._____
5. A. loyalty B. occasional C. hosiery D. bungalow E. undicided 5._____
6. A. efficient B. suberb C. achievement D. bored E. specimen 6._____
7. A. adaquate B. salaries C. utilize D. alcohol E. colonel 7._____
8. A. forcibly B. guardian C. preceeding D. quartile E. quizzes 8._____
9. A. seiges B. unanimous C. ridiculous D. everlasting E. omissions 9._____
10. A. itemized B. ignoramus C. adige D. adieu E. nickel 10._____
11. A. resources B. fileal C. nervous D. logical E. certificate 11._____
12. A. wiring B. turkeys C. morass D. obvious E. bigimmy 12._____
13. A. affirmitive B. noisy C. clothe D. carnage E. perceive 13._____
14. A. ignorant B. literally C. humerists D. business E. awkward 14._____
15. A. thermometer B. tragady C. partisan D. kinsman E. grandiose 15._____
16. A. fundamental B. herald C. delinquent D. kindergarden E. ascertain 16._____
17. A. apropriation B. year's C. vacancy D. enthusiastic E. dormitory 17._____
18. A. crochet B. courtesies C. troup D. occasionally E. spirits 18._____
19. A. typewriting B. inadequate C. legitimate D. fuelless E. restarant 19._____
20. A. tabloux B. cooperage C. wrapped D. tenant E. referring 20._____

KEY (CORRECT ANSWERS)

1. D. consequently
2. E. ambassador
3. D. competition
4. A. conservatory
5. E. undecided
6. B. suburb
7. A. adequate
8. C. preceding OR proceeding
9. A. sieges
10. C. adage
11. B. filial
12. E. bigamy
13. A. affirmative
14. C. humorists
15. B. tragedy
16. D. kindergarten
17. A. appropriation
18. C. troop OR troupe
19. E. restaurant
20. A. tableaux OR tableaus

TEST 2

DIRECTIONS: In each question of the following tests, select the letter of the one MISSPELLED word in each of the listed groups of five (5) words. *PRINT THE LETTER OF THE CORRECT ANSWER IN THE SPACE AT THE RIGHT.*

1. A. loot B. surgery C. breif D. talcum E. Christmas 1.____
2. A. commenced B. congenial C. fatal D. politician E. standerd 2.____
3. A. unbarable B. physician C. potato D. wiring E. adorable 3.____
4. A. error B. regretted C. instetute D. typhoid E. we're 4.____
5. A. merly B. opportunity C. patterns D. unctious E. righteous 5.____
6. A. luxury B. forty C. control D. originally E. intemate 6.____
7. A. plague B. ignorance C. poltrey D. hence E. bruise 7.____
8. A. athletic B. exebition C. leased D. interrupt E. spirits 8.____
9. A. destruction B. prairie C. quartet D. status E. competators 9.____
10. A. triumph B. utility C. loyalty D. antisapte E. crochet 10.____
11. A. lieutenant B. recrute C. thermometer D. quantities E. usefulness 11.____
12. A. wholly B. sitting C. probably D. criticism E. lynche 12.____
13. A. anteque B. galvanized C. mercantile D. academy E. defense 13.____
14. A. kinsman B. declaration C. absurd D. dispach E. patience 14.____
15. A. opportune B. abbuting C. warranted D. refrigerator E. raisin 15.____
16. A. deffered B. principalship C. lovable D. athletic E. conveniently 16.____
17. A. mislaid B. receipted C. skedule D. mission E. whereabouts 17.____
18. A. tuition B. unnatural C. remodel D. consequence E. misdameanor 18.____
19. A. assessment B. advises C. embassys D. border E. leased 19.____
20. A. morale B. legitemate C. infamy D. indebtedness E. technical 20.____

KEY (CORRECT ANSWERS)

1. C. brief
2. E. standard
3. A. unbearable
4. C. institute
5. A. merely
6. E. intimate
7. C. poultry OR paltry
8. B. exhibition
9. E. competition
10. D. anticipate
11. B. recruit
12. E. lynch
13. A. antique
14. D. dispatch
15. B. abutting
16. A. deferred OR differed
17. C. schedule
18. E. misdemeanor
19. C. embassies
20. B. legitimate

TEST 3

DIRECTIONS: In each question of the following tests, select the letter of the one MISSPELLED word in each of the listed groups of five (5) words. *PRINT THE LETTER OF THE CORRECT ANSWER IN THE SPACE AT THE RIGHT.*

1. A. stepfather B. fireman C. loot D. conclusivly E. commodity 1.____
2. A. mislaid B. roommate C. religous D. thesis E. temporary 2.____
3. A. statutes B. malice C. unbridled D. aisle E. cavelry 3.____
4. A. aknowledge B. immensely C. quantities D. erratic E. postponed 4.____
5. A. people's B. foreign C. obsticles D. opportunity E. cordially 5.____
6. A. fragrance B. burgaleries C. clothe D. twins E. herculean 6.____
7. A. warranted B. yoke C. democrat D. parashute E. Bible 7.____
8. A. existance B. enthusiasm C. medal D. sandwiches E. dunce 8.____
9. A. loyalty B. eternal C. chanceler D. psychology E. assessment 9.____
10. A. bungalow B. mutilate C. forcible D. ridiculous E. cawcus 10.____
11. A. lieutenant B. abandoned C. successor D. phisycal E. inquiries 11.____
12. A. nuisance B. coranation C. voluntary D. faculties E. awe 12.____
13. A. indipendance B. notwithstanding C. tariff D. opportune E. accompanying 13.____
14. A. statutes B. rhubarb C. corset D. prurient E. subsedy 14.____
15. A. partisan B. initiate C. colonel D. ilness E. errant 15.____
16. A. acquired B. wrapped C. propriater D. screech E. dune 16.____
17. A. sufrage B. countenance C. fraternally D. undo E. fireman 17.____
18. A. ladies B. chef C. spirituelist D. Sabbath E. itemized 18.____
19. A. ere B. interests C. cheesecloth D. paridoxical E. garish 19.____
20. A. bulletin B. neutral C. porttiere D. discretion E. inconvenienced 20.____

KEY (CORRECT ANSWERS)

1. D. conclusively
2. C. religious
3. E. cavalry
4. A. acknowledge
5. C. obstacles
6. B. burglaries
7. D. parachute
8. A. existence
9. C. chancellor
10. E. caucus
11. D. physical
12. B. coronation
13. A. independence
14. E. subsidy
15. D. illness
16. C. proprietor
17. A. suffrage
18. C. spiritualist
19. D. paradoxical
20. C. portiere

TEST 4

DIRECTIONS: In each question of the following tests, select the letter of the one MISSPELLED word in each of the listed groups of five (5) words. *PRINT THE LETTER OF THE CORRECT ANSWER IN THE SPACE AT THE RIGHT.*

1. A. I'd B. premises C. hysterics D. aparantly E. faculties 1.____
2. A. discipline B. ajurnment C. bachelor D. lose E. wrapped 2.____
3. A. simular B. bulletin C. lovable D. bored E. quizzes 3.____
4. A. attendance B. preparation C. refrigerator D. cafateria E. twelfth 4.____
5. A. inconvenienced B. courtesies C. raisin D. hosiery E. politicean 5.____
6. A. reccommendation B. colonel C. sandwiches D. women's E. undoubtedly 6.____
7. A. technical B. imediately C. temporarily D. dormitory E. voluntary 7.____
8. A. salaries B. abandoned C. consistent D. unconcious E. herald 8.____
9. A. duly B. leer C. emphasise D. vacant E. requisition 9.____
10. A. melancholy B. citrus C. omissions D. bazaar E. derigable 10.____
11. A. acquired B. mercury C. stetistics D. thought E. vassal 11.____
12. A. tempature B. calendar C. series D. gout E. alcohol 12.____
13. A. important B. foreigner C. Australia D. leggend E. rhythm 13.____
14. A. height B. achevement C. monarchial D. axle E. fertile 14.____
15. A. falsity B. prestige C. conquer D. arketecture E. Jerusalem 15.____
16. A. magnifecent B. bacteria C. holly D. diseases E. cellar 16.____
17. A. medicine B. grievous C. beaker D. benefits E. attendents 17.____
18. A. military B. vacancy C. weird D. feudalism E. hybird 18.____
19. A. adopted B. agrigate C. Renaissance D. tournament E. colonies 19.____
20. A. vivisection B. penitentiary C. candadacy D. seer E. Sabbath 20.____

KEY (CORRECT ANSWERS)

1. D. apparently
2. B. adjournment
3. A. similar
4. D. cafeteria
5. E. politician
6. A. recommendation
7. B. immediately
8. D. unconscious
9. C. emphasizes or emphasis
10. E. dirigible
11. C. statistics
12. A. temperature
13. D. legend
14. B. achievement
15. D. architecture
16. A. magnificent
17. E. attendants
18. E. hybrid
19. B. aggregate
20. C. candidacy

TEST 5

DIRECTIONS: In each question of the following tests, select the letter of the one MIS-SPELLED word in each of the listed groups of five (5) words. *PRINT THE LETTER OF THE CORRECT ANSWER IN THE SPACE AT THE RIGHT.*

1. A. acknowledging   B. deligate   C. foliage   D. staid   E. loot   1.____
2. A. gandar   B. losing   C. notwithstanding   D. worlds   E. torrent   2.____
3. A. medal   B. utilize   C. efficiency   D. apricot   E. soliceting   3.____
4. A. museum   B. Christian   C. possesion   D. occasional   E. bored   4.____
5. A. capitol   B. sieze   C. premises   D. fragrance   E. tonnage   5.____
6. A. requisition   B. faculties   C. canon   D. chaufur   E. stomach   6.____
7. A. solemn   B. ascertain   C. I'll   D. chef   E. delinquant   7.____
8. A. parliments   B. distributor   C. voluntary   D. lovable   E. counsel   8.____
9. A. morale   B. democrat   C. rhumatism   D. dormitory   E. leased   9.____
10. A. screech   B. missapropriating   C. courtesies   D. wraith   E. furlough   10.____
11. A. tryst   B. tarriff   C. visible   D. accent   E. contraries   11.____
12. A. dizzy   B. leggings   C. steak   D. compaine   E. interior   12.____
13. A. profit   B. tiranny   C. shocked   D. response   E. innocent   13.____
14. A. freshman   B. vague   C. larsiny   D. ignorant   E. worrying   14.____
15. A. disatesfied   B. jealous   C. unfortunately   D. economical   E. lettuce   15.____
16. A. based   B. primarily   C. condemned   D. accompanied   E. dupped   16.____
17. A. superntendant   B. veil   C. congenial   D. quantities   E. ere   17.____
18. A. unanimous   B. dessert   C. undoubtedly   D. kolera   E. nuisance   18.____
19. A. woman's   B. bolero   C. 'tis   D. Pullman   E. envellop   19.____
20. A. initiate   B. grist   C. pagent   D. mention   E. adieu   20.____

KEY (CORRECT ANSWERS)

1. B. delegate
2. A. gander
3. E. soliciting
4. C. possession
5. B. seize
6. D. chauffeur
7. E. delinquent
8. A. parliaments
9. C. rheumatism
10. B. misappropriating
11. B. tariff
12. D. campaign
13. B. tyranny
14. C. larceny
15. A. dissatisfied
16. E. duped
17. A. superintendent
18. D. cholera
19. E. envelope
20. C. pageant

TEST 6

DIRECTIONS: In each question of the following tests, select the letter of the one MIS-SPELLED word in each of the listed groups of five (5) words. *PRINT THE LETTER OF THE CORRECT ANSWER IN THE SPACE AT THE RIGHT.*

1. A. attach B. voucher C. twins D. assistence E. cordial 1.____
2. A. faculties B. people's C. indetedness D. ignorant E. resource 2.____
3. A. wholly B. apitite C. twelfth D. unauthorized E. embroider 3.____
4. A. certified B. attorneys C. foggy D. potato E. extravigent 4.____
5. A. hysterics B. simelar C. intelligent D. label E. salaries 5.____
6. A. apponants B. we're C. finely D. herald E. continuous 6.____
7. A. cancellation B. athletic C. perminant D. preference E. utilize 7.____
8. A. urns B. zephyr C. tuition D. incidentally E. aquisition 8.____
9. A. kinsaan B. bazaar C. foliage D. wretched E. asassination 9.____
10. A. insignia B. bimonthly C. typewriting D. notariety E. psychology 10.____
11. A. continually B. guild C. vegtable D. vague E. patience 11.____
12. A. desease B. parole C. gallery D. awkward E. you'd 12.____
13. A. border B. warrant C. operated D. economics E. ilegal 13.____
14. A. fatal B. agatation C. obliged D. studying E. resignation 14.____
15. A. ammendment B. promptness C. glimpse D. canon E. tract 15.____
16. A. wholly B. apricot C. destruction D. pappal E. leisure 16.____
17. A. issuing B. rabbid C. unusual D. parasite E. khaki 17.____
18. A. nowadays B. courtesies C. negotiate D. gaurdian E. derrick 18.____
19. A. partisan B. seanse C. vacancy D. fragrance E. corps 19.____
20. A. equipped B. nuisance C. phrenology D. foriegn E. insignia 20.____

KEY (CORRECT ANSWERS)

1. D. assistance
2. C. indebtedness
3. B. appetite
4. E. extravagant
5. B. similar
6. A. opponents
7. C. permanent
8. E. acquisition
9. E. assassination
10. D. notoriety
11. C. vegetable
12. A. disease
13. E. illegal
14. B. agitation
15. A. amendment
16. D. papal
17. B. rabid
18. D. guardian
19. B. eance
20. D. foreign

TEST 7

DIRECTIONS: In each question of the following tests, select the letter of the one MISSPELLED word in each of the listed groups of five (5) words. *PRINT THE LETTER OF THE CORRECT ANSWER IN THE SPACE AT THE RIGHT.*

1. A. frightfully B. mantain C. post office D. specific E. bachelor 1.____
2. A. cease B. turkeys C. woman's D. hustling E. weild 2.____
3. A. expidition B. valuing C. typhoid D. grapevines E. advice 3.____
4. A. balance B. visible C. correspondant D. etc. E. arctic 4.____
5. A. benefit B. arkives C. classified D. inasmuch E. sincerity 5.____
6. A. obedient B. vengeance C. plague D. fascinate E. contageous 6.____
7. A. desicion B. partner C. economy D. piece E. arrogant 7.____
8. A. dyeing B. lightning C. millenary D. undulate E. embarrass 8.____
9. A. strenuous B. isicle C. panel D. suburb E. luxury 9.____
10. A. aisle B. proffer C. people's D. condemed E. morale 10.____
11. A. advising B. recognizing C. seize D. supply E. tradegy 11.____
12. A. intensive B. stationary C. benifit D. equipped E. preferring 12.____
13. A. predjudice B. pervade C. excel D. capitol E. chimera 13.____
14. A. all right B. ninty C. cronies D. nervous E. separate 14.____
15. A. atheletic B. queue C. schedule D. furl E. credible 15.____
16. A. inevitable B. sincerly C. monkeys D. definite E. cynical 16.____
17. A. niece B. accommodate C. loveliness D. reciept E. forcibly 17.____
18. A. cancel B. chagrined C. allies D. playwright E. liutenant 18.____
19. A. pageant B. alcohol C. villian D. Odyssey E. criticize 19.____
20. A. acknowledge B. article C. contemptible D. taciturn E. sovreign 20.____

KEY (CORRECT ANSWERS)

1. B. maintain
2. E. wield
3. A. expedition
4. C. correspondent
5. B. archives
6. E. contagious
7. A. decision
8. C. millinery
9. B. icicle
10. D. condemned
11. E. tragedy
12. C. benefit
13. A. prejudice
14. B. ninety
15. A. athletic
16. B. sincerely
17. D. receipt
18. E. lieutenant
19. C. villain
20. E. sovereign

TEST 8

DIRECTIONS: In each question of the following tests, select the letter of the one MISSPELLED word in each of the listed groups of five (5) words. *PRINT THE LETTER OF THE CORRECT ANSWER IN THE SPACE AT THE RIGHT.*

1. A. incurred   B. cieling   C. strengthen   D. carnage   E. typical   1._____
2. A. twins   B. year's   C. acutely   D. changible   E. facility   2._____
3. A. deliscious   B. enormous   C. likeness   D. witnesses   E. commodity   3._____
4. A. scenes   B. enlargement   C. discretion   D. acknowledging   E. sesion   4._____
5. A. annum   B. strenuous   C. tretchery   D. infamy   E. opporture   5._____
6. A. marmelade   B. loot   C. kinsman   D. crochet   E. hawser   6._____
7. A. sophmore   B. duly   C. across   D. lovable   E. propaganda   7._____
8. A. quantities   B. rickety   C. roommate   D. penetentiary   E. lose   8._____
9. A. interrupt   B. cauldron   C. convienient   D. successor   E. apiece   9._____
10. A. acquire   B. incesent   C. forfeit   D. typewritten   E. dysentery   10._____
11. A. inferred   B. whisle   C. jovial   D. conscript   E. gracious   11._____
12. A. tantalizing   B. ominous   C. conductor   D. duchess   E. telegram   12._____
13. A. reconcile   B. primitive   C. sausy   D. quinine   E. cede   13._____
14. A. immagine   B. viaduct   C. chisel   D. Saturn   E. currant   14._____
15. A. amplify   B. greace   C. cholera   D. perilous   E. theology   15._____
16. A. pursevere   B. deodorize   C. ligament   D. illuminate   E. dropsy   16._____
17. A. cavalier   B. transparent   C. perjury   D. vicinaty   E. navigate   17._____
18. A. postpone   B. dictaphone   C. corral   D. alligator   E. arteficial   18._____
19. A. cannon   B. hospital   C. distilliry   D. righteous   E. secession   19._____
20. A. matrimony   B. digestable   C. scrutiny   D. artisan   E. mediocre   20._____

KEY (CORRECT ANSWERS)

1. B. ceiling
2. D. changeable
3. A. delicious
4. E. session
5. C. treachery
6. A. marmalade
7. A. sophomore
8. D. penitentiary
9. C. convenient
10. B. incessant
11. B. whistle
12. E. telegram
13. C. saucy
14. A. imagine
15. B. grease
16. A. persevere
17. D. vicinity
18. E. artificial
19. C. distillery
20. B. digestible

TEST 9

DIRECTIONS: In each question of the following tests, select the letter of the one MIS-SPELLED word in each of the listed groups of five (5) words. *PRINT THE LETTER OF THE CORRECT ANSWER IN THE SPACE AT THE RIGHT.*

1. A. feirce B. ascent C. allies D. doctor E. coming 1.____
2. A. hopeless B. absense C. foretell D. certain E. similar 2.____
3. A. advise B. muscle C. manual D. provocation E. copywright 3.____
4. A. behooves B. reservoir C. frostbiten D. squalor E. ambuscade 4.____
5. A. systematic B. precious C. tremendos D. insulation E. brilliant 5.____
6. A. significant B. jurisdiction C. libel D. monkies E. legacy 6.____
7. A. dual B. authentic C. serenety D. mechanism E. suburban 7.____
8. A. candel B. dissolution C. laceration D. portend E. pigeon 8.____
9. A. loyalty B. periodic C. presume D. led E. suprano 9.____
10. A. mania B. medicinal C. dungarees D. overwelming E. masquerade 10.____
11. A. pitiful B. latter C. ommitted D. agreement E. reconcile 11.____
12. A. bananna B. routine C. likewise D. indecent E. habitually 12.____
13. A. relieve B. copys C. ninety D. crowded E. electoral 13.____
14. A. adviseable B. illustrative C. financial D. nevertheless E. chimneys 14.____
15. A. prisioner B. immediate C. statistics D. surgeon E. abscond 15.____
16. A. option B. extradite C. comparitive D. jealousy E. illusion 16.____
17. A. handicaped B. assurance C. sympathy D. speech E. dining 17.____
18. A. recommend B. carraige C. disapprove D. independent E. mortgage 18.____
19. A. systematic B. ingenuity C. tenet D. uncanny E. intrigueing 19.____
20. A. arduous B. hideous C. fervant D. companies E. breach 20.____

KEY (CORRECT ANSWERS)

1. A. fierce
2. B. absence
3. E. copyright
4. C. frostbitten
5. C. tremendous
6. D. monkeys
7. C. serenity
8. A. candle
9. E. soprano
10. D. overwhelming
11. C. omitted
12. A. banana
13. B. copies
14. A. advisable
15. A. prisoner
16. C. comparative
17. A. handicapped
18. B. carriage
19. E. intriguing
20. C. fervent

TEST 10

DIRECTIONS: In each question of the following tests, select the letter of the one MIS-SPELLED word in each of the listed groups of five (5) words. *PRINT THE LETTER OF THE CORRECT ANSWER IN THE SPACE AT THE RIGHT.*

1. A. together B. attempt C. loyality D. innocent E. rinse 1.____
2. A. argueing B. emergency C. kindergarten D. religious E. schedule 2.____
3. A. society B. anticipate C. dissatisfy D. responsable E. temporary 3.____
4. A. chaufeur B. grammar C. planned D. dining room E. accurate 4.____
5. A. confidence B. maturity C. aspirations D. evasion E. insurence 5.____
6. A. unnecessary B. dirigible C. transparant D. similar E. appetite 6.____
7. A. treachery B. comedian C. arrest D. recollect E. mistep 7.____
8. A. falsify B. blight C. flexible D. drasticaly E. meddlesome 8.____
9. A. congestion B. publickly C. receipts D. academic E. paralyze 9.____
10. A. possibilities B. undergoes C. consistant D. aggression E. pledge 10.____
11. A. wrist B. welfare C. necessity D. scenery E. tendancy 11.____
12. A. commiting B. accusation C. endurance D. agreeable E. excitable 12.____
13. A. despair B. surgury C. privilege D. appreciation E. journeying 13.____
14. A. cameos B. propaganda C. delicious D. heathen E. interupt 14.____
15. A. relieve B. disappear C. development D. matress E. ninety-nine 15.____
16. A. finally B. bullitin C. doctor D. desirable E. sincerely 16.____
17. A. wrest B. array C. auspices D. sacrafice E. generations 17.____
18. A. liquid B. vegetable C. silence D. familiar E. fasinate 18.____
19. A. tomato B. suspence C. leisure D. license E. permanent 19.____
20. A. characteristic B. soliciting C. repitious D. immediately E. extravagant 20.____

KEY (CORRECT ANSWERS)

1. C. loyalty
2. A. arguing
3. D. responsible
4. A. chauffeur
5. E. insurance
6. C. transparent
7. E. misstep
8. D. drastically
9. B. publicly
10. C. consistent
11. E. tendency
12. A. committing
13. B. surgery
14. E. interrupt
15. D. mattress
16. B. bulletin
17. D. sacrifice
18. E. fascinate
19. B. suspense
20. C. repetitious

EXAMINATION SECTION
TEST 1

DIRECTIONS: In each of the following groups of sentences, one sentence is incorrect because it includes an error in grammar, usage, sentence structure, capitalization, diction, or punctuation. Indicate the INCORRECT sentence.

1. A. Under pressure, many school secretaries may become unnecessarily short and curt with visitors.
   B. She had not hardly opened the school office when she found a long line of mothers waiting to register their children.
   C. The discussion among the three secretaries helped to resolve the problem of responsibility for specific tasks.
   D. The principal said, "All of us are dependent on you for rapid and courteous telephone service."

   1.____

2. A. "Why," she asked, "must I be responsible for training students helpers at the switchboard?"
   B. You must not doubt your ability to learn to prepare payroll reports.
   C. Learning to operate duplicating machines is an important part of a secretary's duties.
   D. I realize the values of promptness and accuracy in the office.

   2.____

3. A. Never permit yourself to become so impersonal in your relationships that you lose your ability to get along with others.
   B. Please take this package to the teacher in room 304.
   C. Each of us has the task of arranging their own desks for quick and efficient work.
   D. I sent the pencils, paper, and books to the chairmen's offices.

   3.____

4. A. Yesterday, the supplies were delivered; today, they must be distributed.
   B. The secretary sat down besides the new pupil to explain how the form was to be completed.
   C. Should you encounter an error made by a teacher on a report, please tell the teacher tactfully of the error.
   D. You may find it wise to proofread all items that you have typed before you remove them from the machine.

   4.____

5. A. Did you understand the relay message to mean that all new secretaries must report for an orientation session?
   B. If you are asked to take dictation, make certain that you have the required items readily at hand.
   C. It is your responsibility to report any bomb threat to the ranking supervisor immediately.
   D. Irregardless of your previous instructions, you are not to permit students to go to the permanent record file.

   5.____

6. A. She is one of those secretaries who is always accurate in her work.
   B. All of us agree that there should be some equitable distribution of office assignments.

   6.____

135

C. As the school secretary picked up the telephone she heard a student shouting "Fire!" at the top of his voice.
D. You must be certain that the principal wishes to see a visitor before you usher the visitor into the principal's office.

7. A. In so far as I am able, I shall attempt to serve all members of the community who enter the school office.
B. The school secretary who had typed the requisition had omitted the identifying number given in the supply list.
C. Her typing was as fast, if not faster than, any secretary he had ever had.
D. In order to complete the payroll, it may become necessary, on occasion, for the school secretary to remain beyond the regular school day.

7.____

8. A. The school secretary with a firm knowledge of school accounts and records is an asset to any school office.
B. The accurate preparation of period attendance reports may enable the city to obtain its proper proportion of state funds.
C. Initiative on the part of the school secretary may result in improvement in the organization and administration of school routine.
D. "I seriously believe," she said, "that if we receive less than six helpers we cannot do the job."

8.____

9. A. As the parent left the office, she said, "How can I ever repay you back for your kindness?"
B. Any money taken from the petty cash fund must be accounted for.
C. The requisitions had to be signed and dated before they could be mailed.
D. Needless to say, I urge you to be prompt and regular in attendance.

9.____

10. A. Because all members of the office staff pitched in and helped, the huge task was completed in an extra ordinarily short period of time.
B. "If it cannot be completed by three o'clock, I am willing to stay overtime," she said.
C. Your typing has improved greatly both in accuracy and in speed.
D. Turning the page, the secretary's eye was attracted to the advertisement for a time-stamping device.

10.____

11. A. The secretary said, "I do not mean to infer that I am displeased with this typewriter."
B. Relatively few of the children who came into the office had been given passes by their teachers.
C. The parent, who had been waiting for a long time before any attention was paid to her, vented her anger on the inconsiderate secretary.
D. The school secretary working in the general office very tactfully urged the teachers to lower their voices.

11.____

12. A. The newly appointed member of the office staff was told that the assistant principal would tell her how to complete the report.
B. If you follow these suggestions, they will teach you self-control and to be tactful.
C. Observing the teacher's difficulty in understanding the pension statement, the school secretary offered to assist her.
D. She was most eager to learn the operation of the duplicating machine.

12.____

13. A. She took the reprimand very badly in that she assumed that it was an attack on her personally rather than on the nature of her work.
    B. By requesting the visitor to wait for a pass, she demonstrated that she was following the rules of the school.
    C. The notice on the bulletin board read: "Any discourtesy to our staff, if reported to the principal, will be greatly appreciated."
    D. May I have your permission to read the announcement over the public address system?

13.____

14. A. You will undoubtedly become proficient as you gain experience.
    B. Have you been greatly effected in preparing the attendance reports by the transit strike?
    C. It is urgent that student monitors be sent to each of the classrooms with the message.
    D. Please keep an exact record of the date, time, and type of each fire drill that we conduct.

14.____

15. A. If you take too much time during the mid-morning break, you place an extra burden on the secretaries who remain in the office.
    B. Please edit and proofread all notices before duplicating them.
    C. I do not anticipate any difficulty in developing the proper touch needed for operation of the electric type writer.
    D. In comparing the work done by the two school secretaries, I must admit that Miss Smith is the fastest typist.

15.____

16. A. In the event that a teacher is absent from school, she is to call the school at 7:30 a.m. or as close to that time as possible.
    B. The notation on the "While You Were Out" slip indicated that Mr. Lane of the board of education had called.
    C. Decisions of these kinds may have to be made by you if no supervisor is available.
    D. What kind of information did the parent request?

16.____

17. A. In answering the telephone, please give the name and borough of the school first.
    B. Why not try arranging the supplies neatly in your desk so that you can reach every item without difficulty?
    C. As she was preparing the list of names of students serving on the school newspaper staff, the secretary asked me how to list two editor-in-chiefs.
    D. Keep a list of printed forms that are in short supply so that we can order the forms we need.

17.____

18. A. The secretary prepared a notice which was put in the mail boxes of all teachers, including yourself.
    B. Do not yield to the temptation to deal with a poorly dressed person in a way which is different from the way in which you treat others.
    C. You will find the envelope directly behind the file folder headed "Correspondence."
    D. May I ask you to double check the totals for each column so that you are certain that the addition is correct.

18.____

19. A. Although the salesman was very persuasive, I refused to let him see the principal while the principal was in conference. 19.____
    B. Don't you think that it would be worth your while to improve the speed and accuracy of your typing?
    C. If the principal has left for the day, be sure to have the administrative assistant check the form before you duplicate it.
    D. We ordered the book before the special circular arrived describing the procedure to be followed.

20. A. The development of friction between co-workers is not inevitable. 20.____
    B. Do not be overly pessimistic about your ability to learn to prepare the period report correctly.
    C. Her manner with the children who come into the office is much too brusque and sharp, but I think that she is basically kind.
    D. The data is correct and, therefore, it may be incorporated into the report.

21. A. The best time to do work requiring full concentration is when the office is quiet. 21.____
    B. She inquired, "Are you going to hand in your report at 3:00 p.m.?"
    C. We should pay full attention to every kind of a written report.
    D. She learned that further practice had had a good effect on her ability to transcribe.

22. A. After brief training, she was ready to accept greater responsibility. 22.____
    B. According to my calendar, your examinations are due today for stencilling.
    C. Let's put aside this kind of work until later.
    D. Strict accuracy is a necessary requisite in record keeping.

23. A. Her desk was orderly, though piled high with folders; furthermore, her supplies were neatly arranged. 23.____
    B. She claims that our filing procedures need revision because they've become so boresome.
    C. "May I ask you, Miss Hawkins," said the principal's secretary, "to come in at once?"
    D. Oddly enough, he had forgotten to reset the school's clock for daylight saving time.

24. A. She had an almost hypnotic fascination for the rhythmical operation of the mimeograph machine. 24.____
    B. "Dr. Franklin, Professor Marlin, and Messrs. Clark, Havens, and Wilson will visit us today," wrote the principal in a memorandum.
    C. She quickly mastered the nomenclature of the supply catalogs.
    D. He informed all personnel not to furnish medicine to any pupil.

25. A. The pupil's account of his lateness is incredible, I will not give him a classroom pass. 25.____
    B. Her willingness to type was due to her desire to learn the forms.
    C. They scheduled their lunch hours in such a way that the switchboard could be covered constantly.
    D. She replenished her supply of clips, staples, bond paper, and pencils.

KEY (CORRECT ANSWERS)

1.	B	11.	A
2.	A	12.	B
3.	C	13.	C
4.	B	14.	B
5.	D	15.	D
6.	A	16.	B
7.	C	17.	C
8.	D	18.	A
9.	A	19.	D
10.	D	20.	D

21. C
22. D
23. B
24. A
25. A

TEST 2

DIRECTIONS: In each of the following groups of sentences, one sentence is incorrect because it includes an error in grammar, usage, sentence structure, capitalization, diction, or punctuation. Indicate the INCORRECT sentence.

1. A. They were thought to be we.
    B. The secretary whom we thought deserved the honor will receive a prize.
    C. The principal herself arranged the new library schedule.
    D. I am sorry to be unable to recommend a monitor for your office.

1.____

2. A. Please lay the carbon paper on the proper shelf.
    B. The principal is expected to return inside of an hour.
    C. I seldom if ever make errors when I type letters.
    D. I feel confident that I am able to do this work accurately and neatly.

2.____

3. A. To Mrs. Andersen have fallen the responsibilities of supply secretary.
    B. The secretary pointed out that all individuals under twenty-one years of age are legally considered minors.
    C. Mrs. Thompson, with her son and daughter, are going to the annual business show.
    D. There are fewer errors in this report than in the last report.

3.____

4. A. One secretary referred to the project as "worthwhile and creative."
    B. I thought this typewriter was hers.
    C. A number of our secretarial staff is going on vacation soon.
    D. These typewriters are very sturdy: they are made from strong metal and unbreakable plastic.

4.____

5. A. "I know," he said, "that you can finish this project today."
    B. I found Miss Jones the most cooperative of the two secretaries.
    C. My sister who works at Public School 73 lives in Manhattan.
    D. Our school secretary is always appropriately attired and well groomed.

5.____

6. A. The letter has lain on the principal's desk all day, waiting for his signature.
    B. We believe that three-quarters of the work is done.
    C. She said, "Neither you nor I am responsible for that error."
    D. Let me speak to whomever is waiting for the assistant principal.

6.____

7. A. How disappointing it was to hear him say, "Your bus has left!"
    B. It was a dark, dismal, dreary, December day.
    C. Do you know any alumnae of a women's college?
    D. It is imperative that you enunciate your words clearly when you use the telephone.

7.____

8. A. "Will you have time," he inquired, "to prepare transcripts for our college-bound graduates?"
    B. You work more efficiently than her because you anticipate and avoid time-consuming trifles.

8.____

C. Questions regarding procedure should be referred to a disinterested expert, should they not?
D. The chairmen of the health education, foreign language, mathematics, and English departments requested supply requisition forms.

9. A. The instant the principal began to dictate, the bell rang, interrupting his train of thought.   9.____
   B. This is one of those machines that are constantly breaking down.
   C. She asked me whether I would remain a few additional minutes to check her report.
   D. A well-organized schedule makes it possible to complete more work with less helpers.

10. A. Teachers' letter boxes should not be filled in such a way as to create difficulty in removing individual 3" x 5" cards.   10.____
    B. By being courteous, emotional outbursts can be avoided in discussions with irate parents.
    C. Her transcribing was interrupted by the whirring, often much too loud, of the engines in the street.
    D. In business letters, correct phrasing, as well as the avoidance of circumlocution, is a virtue.

11. A. Listening intently to the heated discussion at the conference, Laura forgot to take notes; consequently, the minutes were incomplete.   11.____
    B. If I were going to prepare the payroll report, I should begin as long in advance as possible.
    C. She asked the student to bring the book to the principal.
    D. The secretaries agreed among themselves that each would do a certain amount of correspondence.

12. A. Ida had two tasks; namely, tabulating data and forwarding them to the assistant superintendent.   12.____
    B. Your introduction to the members of the staff has been a pleasant experience, has it not.
    C. "Between you and me, I can hardly tolerate that teacher anyhow," the angry mother confided.
    D. Keeping the office windows fully closed may adversely affect secretaries' efficiency.

13. A. From the tone of the letter, it was easy to imply that the writer was grateful.   13.____
    B. We devised other means of communication since telephone extensions were nonexistent.
    C. The preparation of circulars and attendance reports requires considerable care.
    D. "Please direct me to room 205," said the visitor. "I have an appointment with Mr. Jones."

14. A. An efficient school secretary in punctual, precise, and conscientious.   14.____
    B. For a beginner, she gave a credulous performance on the piano.
    C. I believe we had fewer pupils in the third grade last year.
    D. Are you prepared to take dictation from the principal when he calls you?

15. A. I cannot help but congratulating you for the manner in which you handle the switchboard.
     B. This computer is broken; that hard drive is in need of repairs.
     C. Hurray! Here comes our school band!
     D. Having misplaced her key, the teacher borrowed one from the secretary.

16. A. Please deliver the message to either Miss Spring or her.
     B. I believe that ten dollars is not sufficient for the special type of paper you need.
     C. The most appreciated gift was the diaries you obtained for us.
     D. Our government found it necessary to discourage emigration to this country.

17. A. "What is the correct answer," she asked, "to question one on page 14 in the <u>Secretary's Manual</u>?"
     B. My sister Joan called on the phone to relay the important message.
     C. Please bring this material to the office of the custodian of the school.
     D. All secretaries should be aware of and familiar with the rules of indexing.

18. A. A majority of the members have promised to vote for Mr. Randolph.
     B. The work has been carefully laid out for you; you should have very little difficulty.
     C. His new book is as well written, though less exciting than, his previous book.
     D. Either you or she is the writer of this note and I doubt that it is she.

19. A. Will you please ship the books to us as soon as possible?
     B. A call was placed by Superintendent Donovan to the principal of the school.
     C. A strikeover is when a typist retypes a letter or number on top of the original incorrect one.
     D. The committee which the principal appointed consisted of three people: Mrs. Jones, a teacher; Robert; and Jane.

20. A. I was too greatly relieved to be able to say anything.
     B. These insignia date back to ancient Roman times.
     C. We observed a strange phenomenon; the house seemed to sway in the wind and to tremble like a leaf.
     D. It would be much more preferable if you were no longer seen in his company.

21. A. Please send me this data at your earliest convenience.
     B. The loss of their material proved a severe handicap.
     C. My principal objection to this plan is that it is impracticable.
     D. The doll has lain in the rain all evening.

22. A. I had expected to see my brother.
     B. He expected to have seen his brother.
     C. I hoped to see you do better.
     D. It was his duty to assist our friend.

23. A. The reason why I am writing to you is that I wish to avoid further misunderstanding.
     B. These kind of arguments always cause hard feelings.
     C. Regardless of your decision, I shall have to go.
     D. I have only twenty pupils in this class.

24. A. Which is the youngest of the two sisters?
     B. I am determined to finish the work before Saturday.
     C. It is difficult to see why the problems are not correctly solved.
     D. I have never met a more interesting person.

25. A. Located on a mountainside with a babbling brook beside the door, it was a dream palace.
     B. Blessed are they that have not seen and yet have believed.
     C. The customs in that part of the country are much different than I expected.
     D. Politics, even in towns of small population, has always attracted ambitious young lawyers.

KEY (CORRECT ANSWERS)

1. B
2. B
3. C
4. C
5. B

6. D
7. B
8. B
9. D
10. B

11. C
12. B
13. A
14. B
15. A

16. D
17. C
18. C
19. C
20. D

21. A
22. B
23. B
24. A
25. C

TEST 3

DIRECTIONS: In each of the following groups of sentences, one of the four sentences is faulty in grammar, punctuation, or capitalization. Select the INCORRECT sentence in each case.

1. A. If you had stood at home and done your homework, you would not have failed in arithmetic.
   B. Her affected manner annoyed every member of the audience.
   C. How will the new law affect our income taxes?
   D. The plants were not affected by the long, cold winter, but they succumbed to the drought of summer.

   1.____

2. A. He is one of the most able men who have been in the Senate.
   B. It is he who is to blame for the lamentable mistake.
   C. Haven't you a helpful suggestion to make at this time?
   D. The money was robbed from the blind man's cup.

   2.____

3. A. The amount of children in this school is steadily increasing.
   B. After taking an apple from the table, she went out to play.
   C. He borrowed a dollar from me.
   D. I had hoped my brother would arrive before me.

   3.____

4. A. Whom do you think I hear from every week?
   B. Who do you think is the right man for the job?
   C. Who do you think I found in the room?
   D. He is the man whom we considered a good candidate for the presidency.

   4.____

5. A. Quietly the puppy laid down before the fireplace.
   B. You have made your bed; now lie in it.
   C. I was badly sunburned because I had lain too long in the sun.
   D. I laid the doll on the bed and left the room.

   5.____

6. A. Sailing down the bay was a thrilling experience for me.
   B. He was not consulted about your joining the club.
   C. This story is different than the one I told you yesterday.
   D. There is no doubt about his being the best player.

   6.____

7. A. He maintains there is but one road to world peace.
   B. It is common knowledge that a child sees much he is not supposed to see.
   C. Much of the bitterness might have been avoided if arbitration had been resorted to earlier in the meeting.
   D. The man decided it would be advisable to marry a girl somewhat younger than him.

   7.____

8. A. We have received complaints to the effect that the school's clocks are not synchronized.
   B. My telephone is busier than the others, and so why don't they help me out?
   C. If you had mislaid Mr. Harris' file, would you not have informed the principal immediately?
   D. Please distribute these newly-arrived pension booklets among all the teachers.

   8.____

9. A. One should partake in the orientation discussion and heed the council of one's co-workers.
    B. A general circular was drawn up to correct misunderstanding created by the poorly-worded notice on the bulletin board.
    C. We divide teachers' checks into two alphabetized groups for equitable distribution.
    D. Her initiative has led to a streamlining of cumbersome routines.

10. A. We have just begun to assemble the figures for the period attendance report.
    B. She reports promptly to her assigned station during fire drills.
    C. The person who telephoned insisted on speaking directly to the principal.
    D. "Have you decided, he asked," to prepare the calendar for the remainder of the term?"

11. A. Give this message to whomever you think is a reliable monitor.
    B. You are not allowed to send pupils out of the building without the principal's permission.
    C. The postman placed the mail, tied with strong cord, in front of the time clock.
    D. We mailed notices to no fewer than 280 parents.

12. A. She is reluctantly seeking a transfer because she is going to move.
    B. Miss Wilson, when did we conduct our last shelter area drill?
    C. Since no monitor was available, Miss Foster delivered the message herself.
    D. I'd like an appointment to a school in the east side.

13. A. The information acquired by the school secretary who types observation reports must remain confidential.
    B. You should be impartial to all without sacrificing your friendly approach.
    C. The mail was sorted without they're having to take time from preparing the report.
    D. Your desk will have to be moved while the repairman is working on the ceiling.

14. A. She sent a copy of "How Good Are Our Schools?" reprinted from American Education.
    B. It is long past the time the bell should have rang.
    C. She counted twenty one-dollar bills in the petty cash reserve.
    D. The reason he returned the stencil was that he had found too many errors.

15. A. Dr. Smith, professor of American literature, was the principal speaker.
    B. "Which one of you," asked the principal, "prepared this report?"
    C. There are distinct differences between shorthand, type writing and filing.
    D. I intend to devote the balance of the day to the preparation of the reports.

16. A. Either the librarian or the pupils are wrong.
    B. "Who," asked the principal, "said, 'Correct practice makes perfect'?"
    C. We have the supplies in this cabinet: letterheads, onionskin paper, envelopes, carbon paper, and pencils.
    D. Walking through the corridor, a fire extinguisher came into view.

17. A. The two secretaries entered the lunch room and sat besides us. 17.____
    B. The secretary's success is due to her conscientiousness.
    C. If you find the papers, please let me know about it; but you are certain to have to hunt for them.
    D. I am able to change a typewriter ribbon and to make minor typewriter adjustments.

18. A. The choice of a typewriter is difficult, there are many excellent ones on the market today. 18.____
    B. We have sold an unusually large number of pens in the school store.
    C. Our principal constantly emphasizes punctuality and excellent attendance.
    D. What do you think the effect of the decision will be?

19. A. The last carton of the new envelopes have just been opened. 19.____
    B. The secretary inquired, "Did you hear him ask, 'Who are you?'"
    C. Instead of a 2 and a 7 she had typed two 4's.
    D. She might — and according to plans, should — have completed the project.

20. A. This here typewriter is the one that is not working well. 20.____
    B. I believe that it's time for the bell to ring.
    C. Mr. Clark called us, Evelyn and me, into his office.
    D. Jean and I can distribute the mail before noon.

21. A. Many a clerk and stenographer has become an efficient school secretary. 21.____
    B. The data was assembled by three of our secretaries who served on the committee.
    C. I don't know, Mr. Thompson, where your secretary is.
    D. She was typing the letters accurately and rapidly, of course.

22. A. I do not say exactly that these stories are not true; I only say that I do not believe them. 22.____
    B. My old fountain pen, which never leaked or clogged, is broken and I can use it no further.
    C. Compare the quality of our papers with any other papers in the same price range. There is just no comparison.
    D. Today's news, in the words of a famous Frenchman, is in yesterday's newspaper; tomorrow's, in today's.

23. A. She objected to his reading comics and told him to put it away. 23.____
    B. The patient said that the doctor had ordered him to lie down every day after dinner for two hours and that he had, in fact, lain down for more than three hours.
    C. We are likely to run out of money before our vacation is over, and we shall have to borrow some from our friends.
    D. We are confident that you will appoint whomever is best suited for the position.

24. A. "Age is like love: it cannot be hid." –Thomas Dekker 24.____
    B. The question Mary refused to answer was: Did you see Mr. Clark actually leave the building?
    C. This information, namely, that we are going out of business, is accurate.
    D. The Joneses' house is in excellent condition because Mr. and Mrs. Jones take such good care of it.

25. A. He, not she, is the one to go because he is better prepared than her; thus he can do the job as well as she and we can be sure that it will be done properly.
    B. She had no sooner entered the office and begun to type than the bell announced the first coffee break of the day.
    C. While there has been considerable scholarly interest in the subject, there have been hardly any scientific experiments of any value in the field.
    D. I played the song "Getting To Know You" from the record "The King and I."

25.____

KEY (CORRECT ANSWERS)

1.	A	11.	A
2.	D	12.	D
3.	A	13.	C
4.	C	14.	B
5.	A	15.	D
6.	C	16.	D
7.	D	17.	A
8.	B	18.	A
9.	A	19.	A
10.	C	20.	A

21. B
22. C
23. D
24. B
25. A

EXAMINATION SECTION
TEST 1

DIRECTIONS: In each of the following groups of sentences, there are three sentences which are correct and one which is incorrect because it contains an error in grammar, usage, diction, or punctuation. Indicate the INCORRECT sentence. *PRINT THE LETTER OF THE CORRECT ANSWER IN THE SPACE AT THE RIGHT.*

1. A. Take one of these books which are to be discarded because it has no value any more.
    B. Although the period has lasted for more than thirty minutes, the students are not tired and can do much more work.
    C. Williams has a most unique idea for the school play, and he plans to discuss it with his teacher.
    D. After cleaning the house, my mother lay in the hammock for an hour; then she went shopping.

    1.____

2. A. Sunrise High School, with an enrollment of 1,200 boys and 1,100 girls, is the largest in the state.
    B. I was pleased with his visiting me in the hospital as I was lonely and depressed at the time.
    C. To type with your feet spread out in all directions is considered to be an example of poor typewriting technique.
    D. First-class furs like first-class diamonds are very expensive; both the initial cost and the year-to-year upkeep require a great deal of money.

    2.____

3. A. Not having received a reply to my letter of June 8, I am writing again to ask if anything is wrong.
    B. She asked, "Whom does Mr. Jones feel should have won the typewriting medal?"
    C. Strawberries and cream is a perfect summer dessert, and I have asked my mother to serve the dish frequently.
    D. Either Mary or the boys have broken the window, and I mean to find out immediately before they do further damage.

    3.____

4. A. Of the ladies present at the meeting, three were chosen to be delegates to the annual convention to be held the following May.
    B. The reason I succeeded is that I prepared thoroughly for the test.
    C. I heard her say that the window was broken by the ball and damaged the vase in the living room.
    D. They have been chosen for two reasons—namely, because they are intelligent and because they are conscientious.

    4.____

5. A. Latin, French, and English, in that order, were my favorite subjects in high school.
    B. Since a stay of execution has not been received from the governor, the murderer must be hanged at midnight.
    C. Knowing that you want an immediate answer, I suggest that you send your request to Mr. Smith or to whoever is in charge of such matters.
    D. We ordered pencils and typewriter ribbons whichever were available from the stationer on the corner.

    5.____

6. A. Business was not good; and becoming very irritated, the partners decided to close the store for the day.
   B. I am pleased with your work — work that shows through preparation and in your typewriting ability.
   C. The house was low and long and appeared to be newly built.
   D. This office is often used by salesmen who have nothing better to do, and especially by unsuccessful salesmen.

   6.___

7. A. Reading this well-written book was a never-to-be forgotten experience; I was both repelled and drawn toward the hero.
   B. I can hardly realize that in two weeks I shall be in Europe. The reason is that I have never traveled before.
   C. I want four only, but I will take five or six if you insist.
   D. Mrs. Jones plans to speak with Sally about her poor grades. The girl failed two subjects last month.

   7.___

8. A. Strictly speaking, he cannot be considered a good base ball player — or, for that matter, a good tennis player.
   B. To learn to type well, you should practice daily; to acquire high speed in shorthand, you should practice constantly.
   C. The teachers' committee consisted of Dr. Smith, the principal, Mr. Jones, the program committee chairman, Mrs. Greene, the senior grade adviser, and the administrative assistant.
   D. His secretary and Girl Friday was the most efficient worker he had ever hired, and he was delighted with her.

   8.___

9. A. There were but two of us left after examinations had been graded.
   B. Neither the two bushes nor the elm tree was damaged by the hurricane.
   C. "Did you go to the office?", Mary asked. "No," Sally replied, "and I don't intend to."
   D. The engine as well as the fenders and the wheels was severely damaged, and neither you nor I am prepared to say how much the repair bill will be.

   9.___

10. A. I observed that the house was one of those rambling old mansions that one often sees in Southern towns.
    B. By concentrating on spelling while I am learning how to type, I am putting my time to better use.
    C. Please repeat the sentence again because none of the children in the rear heard you.
    D. The police have arrested three men: John Winters, 27, Brooklyn; Timothy Flynn, 26, Brooklyn; and Sheldon Young, 26, Queens.

    10.___

11. A. "I have laid the book down," she said. "I shall now go to sleep."
    B. The policeman, not the gangsters, merits our approval despite the fact that crime is made to be so attractive on television.
    C. "Did you finish your composition yet?" Sally asked. "No," Jane replied.
    D. Where can I find out who wrote, "What you don't know would make a great book"?

    11.___

12. A. I read in a book that boys and girls today are taller and heavier than their parents were at the same age. How interesting!
    B. John said that from where he was sitting in the ball park, he could hardly see the batter and the pitcher.
    C. He expects to be graduated from Morningside High School in January instead of June as he has been taking extra summer courses.
    D. Speaking of employment, have many new jobs been created on Long Island as a result of all the industries which have settled there during the past five years?

    12.____

13. A. I have risen at five o'clock in the morning for the past twenty years, and I am still in excellent physical condition.
    B. I have laid the letter on my employer's desk several times, but he still has not signed it.
    C. We felt that if he would have tried harder, he might have passed the examination.
    D. I am angry with John principally because I am angry at the comments he made at the rally last night.

    13.____

14. A. I met a friend of father's the other day in Boland and Ryan's suburban store.
    B. Less men were hurt this year than last because of the intensive safety precautions which have been introduced.
    C. During several months — that is, June, July, and August — school is closed.
    D. We need all types of skills in our office — for example stenographers, typists, IBM operators, duplicator operators, and typist-clerks.

    14.____

15. A. The paper says that civil liberties is the principal topic of conversation in Washington today.
    B. I do not know why — but perhaps I shouldn't try to find out at this time.
    C. I would have preferred to do nothing until he came, so I decided to lie down.
    D. As I was entering the office, I heard a bell clang right behind me, which gave me a bad fright.

    15.____

16. A. As I went deeper and deeper into the forest, the light became dimmer and dimmer.
    B. Did he actually say, "I can't do a thing for you"? I can imagine him being so ungrateful.
    C. After he had seen the play OKLAHOMA (which he had been told in advance was excellent), he decided to go to the theater much more often.
    D. Bill Carlton did not go to college, which shocked his family and astonished his friends because Bill was a really good student.

    16.____

17. A. If Tom had worked all summer in a camp or in a restaurant, he might have saved enough money to buy a car.
    B. I am not sure which typewriter is liked better, the Royal or the IBM Selectric; and I plan, therefore, to look into the matter further.
    C. We stopped at John's house to see if his trophy was different from Mark's trophy.
    D. Tom said that he was going over to Sally's house after the school dance and that we should not expect him home until midnight.

    17.____

18. A. Tom never has and never will obtain the grades required for admission to Harvard.   18.____
    B. The rain fell harder and harder as I walked away from home.
    C. "There is nothing to worry about dear," her mother answered quietly. "What a fuss you do get into! Heavens! Now take the nice medicine."
    D. The union leader, whom it was believed all the men admired, was, in fact, very much hated by most of them.

19. A. You had better not stay too long or you will get into trouble—unless, of course, you just don't care.   19.____
    B. His latest book The Psychology of Mental Life was published in 1991. Have you read his other books?
    C. The clerk whom I thought to be the best was, in actuality, the worst.
    D. He said that he sold: typewriters, adding machines, mail equipment, and time clocks.

20. A. There was danger of the enemy attacking from the rear and destroying our army before we could bring up the necessary reserves.   20.____
    B. There were approximately ten applicants in the office waiting to be interviewed for the job.
    C. He acts, it seems to me, as though he were guilty.
    D. We have studied John Smith's, William Wilson's, and Tom Blake's claims; and we feel quite sure that they will soon be settled.

21. A. He is a person who pleases you the moment you meet him, so that you want to be with him and to know him better.   21.____
    B. He had no love for, nor confidence in, his employer.
    C. First type the letter and then you should put it in the envelope.
    D. His salary was lower than a typist's, but he did not care because there were excellent opportunities for advancement.

22. A. I typed this letter – you may not believe this, but it is true – in four minutes.   22.____
    B. "It is clear (the message read) that the Muscle Shoals development is but a small part of the potential public usefulness of the entire Tennessee River."– D.E. Lilienthal
    C. Shaw made his first plunge into controversy: he rose to his feet, shaking with nerves and heard himself speaking.
    D. After the reading of the will, he opened up the strong box and divided up the money among the relatives present.

23. A. Dissatisfaction with the theoretical bases and practical workings of the general property tax has given rise to two movements of tax reform.   23.____
    B. Let the book lie on the table.
    C. Since the department is reducing its number of employees is not proof that they are not needed.
    D. Who do you think will be selected for the position?

24. A. Application of the principles discovered during those experiments have been of great value to mankind.   24.____
    B. Every one of the editorial assistants proved his worth without exception.
    C. State regulation of morals aids in the protection of the family.
    D. Working when one is tired does not yield the best results.

25.
A. We learned that there was more than ten people present at the conference.
B. Every one of the employees is able to lift the carton.
C. Neither the registrar nor the secretary is in the office today.
D. The administrative assistant stated that any office assistant who stayed overtime tonight would get a half-day off next month.

25._____

KEY (CORRECT ANSWERS)

1.	C		11.	C
2.	D		12.	B
3.	B		13.	C
4.	C		14.	B
5.	D		15.	D
6.	B		16.	B
7.	A		17.	D
8.	C		18.	A
9.	C		19.	D
10.	C		20.	A

21. C
22. D
23. C
24. A
25. A

TEST 2

DIRECTIONS: In each of the following groups of sentences, there are three sentences which are correct and one which is incorrect because it contains an error in grammar, usage, diction, or punctuation. Indicate the INCORRECT sentence. *PRINT THE LETTER OF THE CORRECT ANSWER IN THE SPACE AT THE RIGHT.*

1. A. I read political science books as a kind of a duty, not for pleasure.
   B. You needn't go to all that expense for me.
   C. It will be extremely interesting to note the varied reactions of the other participants.
   D. Please do not be angry with me, because it really was not my fault.

   1.____

2. A. We go there by boat and return by train.
   B. He wrote home for his bathing trunks, tennis racket, and set of golf clubs.
   C. Take me to his home, and I will tell him myself.
   D. The autobiography of George Bernard Shaw by Ernest Jones was assigned for reading by my English teacher.

   2.____

3. A. Everyone was given his fair share.
   B. If the river will rise much higher, we may have a flood.
   C. There were, in the early years of this century, many more horses than automobiles.
   D. Either your enunciation is faulty or I am hard of hearing.

   3.____

4. A. The boy assured his teacher that he would pass the tests with ease.
   B. Every person in these two buildings has to meet their responsibilities.
   C. Thunderstorms will invariably follow a lengthy hot spell.
   D. I believe the boy to be him.

   4.____

5. A. I lay it on the bench before I left.
   B. She wrung the clothes before she bought a washing machine.
   C. We have drunk all the water.
   D. The wind has blown like this all night.

   5.____

6. A. I like Shakespeare's HAMLET better than any of his plays.
   B. The roads are in poor condition because of the torrential rains.
   C. They robbed the child.
   D. They have stolen my cash.

   6.____

7. A. If the winner of the contest were here, I would give him his medal.
   B. I hope my son graduates junior high school next June.
   C. Now is the time to make sure that we have beaten that team.
   D. We believe that those books are up to date.

   7.____

8. A. Be careful that you do not slip on that oily surface.
   B. I hope to be able to take notes during his worthwhile lecture.
   C. I think that phenomena is worth photographing.
   D. It occurred in the 1960s, not during the 1950s.

   8.____

9. A. New York is larger than any city in Europe.
    B. Just as we reached the boat landing, the weather changed.
    C. Coming around the curve, the large house was seen.
    D. Generally speaking, my daughter is a good student.

10. A. Place the children's toys above the others.
    B. It was more unique that I thought it would be.
    C. It was my opinion, albeit an erroneous one, that he was the best swimmer on the team.
    D. The typewriter's ribbon was frayed.

11. A. The chances are that Ted's relatives believe in his honesty.
    B. I am glad that you think this was so.
    C. Give it to the club to which my grandmother belongs.
    D. I am in New York for ten years.

12. A. I have heard that he is never returning.
    B. In the last century it was especially fashionable to dress in that manner.
    C. This data, in my opinion, is incorrect.
    D. It is a highly selective procedure which must be followed.

13. A. She sat besides me on the couch.
    B. Billy is the best Spanish scholar of the three boys.
    C. It is gratifying to know that the city school system's strengths are being publicized.
    D. I do not have very much faith in his changing his mind.

14. A. I think that he should be feeling somewhat better.
    B. Do as she does if you want to do it correctly.
    C. I am surely glad that he was able to pass the test.
    D. Hide it some place.

15. A. He seemed to be possessed by an evil spirit.
    B. I think that his point of view is different from mine, but I still believe that I am correct.
    C. I agree to the new plan, but I disagree with him in regard to how it is to be accomplished.
    D. He has the natural desire to be independent from his parents.

16. A. Whenever she went to school she learned a lot.
    B. We had hoped to be on time, but we were late.
    C. My greatest fear, however, was overcome at the last moment.
    D. The two painters' works were displayed at the gallery.

17. A. The check from the Treasury Department will arrive on Monday, January 23.
    B. James was not sure that it was Jane and me at the party.
    C. I do not know if the search for William and her has been made.
    D. There were many accidents on the highway, but the toll was less than had been anticipated.

18. A. A baby girl was just what we wanted.
    B. His vote was the larger of the two candidates.
    C. That boy had neither money or influence, and I do not know what chances of success he had.
    D. I may lie down on that bed if I get tired.

18.____

19. A. He doesn't live too far from his friend's home.
    B. The northeast was covered with snow.
    C. Let's cut it into six portions so that we can each have a piece.
    D. The boy did six days' work.

19.____

20. A. It was in first-class condition, and I decided to keep it.
    B. It was a highly polished piece of jewelry.
    C. The twins, not their little brother, has the measles.
    D. That is the most important document in the history of our country.

20.____

21. A. Medical training in Greece has been modernized, and the younger doctors have either studied in the United States or Europe.
    B. He will not bring the car here without my telling him.
    C. He is as tall as, if not taller than, the teacher,
    D. If one is asked to count from one to five inclusive, he should count as follows: one, two, three, four, five.

21.____

22. A. The leader of the movement is Mr. Harold L. Parne, Esq.
    B. He expects to be graduated from college next month.
    C. If one lives in Florida one day and in Iceland the next, he is certain to feel the change in temperature.
    D. He is the one of the boys who is always on time.

22.____

23. A. Since only one in the jury responded to the foreman's question, he looked at them inquiringly.
    B. According to an old adage, every dog has its day.
    C. It was I whom he wanted to sing.
    D. Now that the stress of examinations and interviews are over, we can all relax for a while.

23.____

24. A. The arrival of the letter was prior to that of the package.
    B. If you convey this suggestion back to your committee, we shall obtain a solution to our problem.
    C. They all looked different after their return from Vietnam.
    D. Illiteracy is the condition of the man who cannot read or write.

24.____

25. A. Do you think we have paid too much? too little?
    B. Neither John nor I am to receive the reward.
    C. The farmer lost nearly one hundred cattle in the fire.
    D. We are making fewer mistakes with the new calculating machine.

25.____

KEY (CORRECT ANSWERS)

1. A
2. D
3. B
4. B
5. A

6. A
7. B
8. C
9. C
10. B

11. D
12. C
13. A
14. D
15. D

16. A
17. B
18. C
19. B
20. C

21. A
22. A
23. D
24. B
25. A

TEST 3

DIRECTIONS: In each of the following groups of sentences, one sentence is incorrect because it includes an error in grammar, usage, sentence structure, capitalization, diction, or punctuation. Indicate the INCORRECT sentence. *PRINT THE LETTER OF THE CORRECT ANSWER IN THE SPACE AT THE RIGHT.*

1.
   A. Her poor posture made taking dictation a fatiguing chore.
   B. The secretary promptly notified the principal of the fire for which she was highly praised.
   C. She makes too frequent use of correction fluid when she types stencils.
   D. Old records are sometimes kept in a basement storeroom.

2.
   A. She learned the uses of punctuation marks from one of the dictionary's appendixes.
   B. The administrative assistant acted as principal in the latter's absence.
   C. You see, you did mail the letter to yourself!
   D. We are impressed by her exemplary performance and industry; they are a stimulant to us to do better work.

3.
   A. The rotation of duties and responsibilities among the secretaries are highly desirable.
   B. The school secretary must remember to maintain contact with teachers assigned to the Board of Education.
   C. She could not operate the electric typewriter because she had not plugged it in.
   D. Eleanor utilized a postal scale to determine the cost of mailing the parcel.

4.
   A. Please list the names of alumnae from the year 1963 on.
   B. Her filing went like clockwork because of the prior alphabetizing of the folders.
   C. She let the phone ring for awhile, but when she finally answered, the line was dead.
   D. The secretary's merits were duly noted in the principal's report.

5.
   A. At closing time, one should not be short tempered with long-winded visitors.
   B. The eraser was lost after it had lain alongside the typewriter.
   C. Her spelling was as acceptable as theirs, if not more acceptable.
   D. We ordered many copies of Webster's new International dictionary from federal funds.

6.
   A. For the sake of expediency, we divided the work between the four of us.
   B. She quickly learnt to use a comptometer.
   C. Miss Smith would rather take dictation than operate the switchboard.
   D. The dimensions of the envelope determine the quantity of matter that may be enclosed.

7.
   A. Joan's suggestion for recording absences, though untried, seems practicable.
   B. The expression, "Thanking you in advance," is unacceptable in up-to-date correspondence.
   C. She informed latecomers not to feel badly because the snowstorm would be accepted as a valid excuse.
   D. The school secretary was pleased that the courses she had taken were relevant to her work.

8. A. He was extremely kind to me yesterday.
    B. I talked to him in regard to the subscription.
    C. They were so good to me.
    D. The teacher spoke clear and emphatic.

    8.____

9. A. Our vacation is over, I am sorry to say.
    B. It is so dark that I can't hardly see.
    C. Either you or I am right; we cannot both be right.
    D. After it had lain in the rain all night, it was not fit for use again.

    9.____

10. A. When either or both habits become fixed, the student improves.
    B. Neither his words nor his action was justifiable.
    C. A calm almost always comes before a storm.
    D. The gallery with all its pictures were destroyed.

    10.____

11. A. Next summer I shall either travel by plane or by boat down to Bermuda.
    B. The reason Tom won the award is that he studied hard.
    C. Undoubtedly the best scene in the play occurs when the son confronts his mother.
    D. History is the record of events that have happened.

    11.____

12. A. John was invited to spend a week at the camp.
    B. My failure was due to the poor method of study I employed at that time.
    C. When I left home, I was only fifteen years old.
    D. We imply from your remarks that you think him guilty.

    12.____

13. A. The advantages of such an arrangement enables the teachers to plan her work more efficiently.
    B. Typing skill is the result merely of the acquisition of a number of habits.
    C. We are more likely to catch cold in overheated rooms than in chilly ones.
    D. Both political parties promise to balance the budget if and when they are elected to office.

    13.____

14. A. They have neither the patience nor the skill necessary to solve these problems.
    B. This is the only decision that can be reached: either you or I are right.
    C. You should lend your book to the student who you think will enjoy reading it.
    D. The Red Cross is doing its utmost to provide medical supplies for the flood areas.

    14.____

15. A. The driver sustained internal injuries.
    B. It is the only textbook of its kind that has, is, or may be published.
    C. Thinking speaking and writing are closely related learnings.
    D. Most of us recognize good English when we hear it or read it.

    15.____

16. A. This sort of emergency always has its exciting moments.
    B. A tragic play is when the action ends unhappily.
    C. The committee adjourned sine die and went to their homes for a much needed rest.
    D. It is essential that you be on the alert at all times.

    16.____

17. A. The reason he was late getting to work was because he overslept.
    B. As we read the daily newspaper headlines, a feeling of despair overwhelms us.
    C. His gentle speech is no proof that he is kind.
    D. Shall we lay the book on the table?

17.____

18. A. We want to travel extensively and have new experiences.
    B. Charles is my brother, James being my cousin.
    C. His teacher is one person in whom he can confide.
    D. The skater suddenly lost control and crashed into the rail.

18.____

19. A. Because he was sympathetic and tolerant, most people respected him.
    B. What are the principal points to be emphasized in the conduct of drill practice?
    C. The lecturer called attention to the beginning of the movement and how it ended.
    D. The average citizen has far more civic power than he realizes.

19.____

20. A. The committee has done their best to raise the money necessary to build the new club house.
    B. He was neither willing nor able to pay the exorbitant fee.
    C. We all want to be happy, and we want our fellow men to be happy.
    D. If ours were a totalitarian society, we would probably limit the number of pupils admitted to colleges.

20.____

21. A. The filling-out of the application blank took up one third of his time.
    B. The talent for brevity is given to few politicians!
    C. Dashing to the front window, the parade came into view.
    D. Each day this newspaper prints a summary of up-to-the-minute news on the front page.

21.____

22. A. Because of his ability as a leader, he was undoubtedly the man for the job.
    B. Not only were they disappointed but also angry.
    C. If one is to learn French well one must speak it regularly.
    D. The most famous collection of prayers known to history is the Book of Psalms.

22.____

23. A. We planned to stay a week in at Rocky Landing.
    B. The bus driver agreed to take as many as wanted to go.
    C. Any man may vote, be he rich or poor.
    D. The teacher assigned three of us, John, Sam, and I, to help with the arrangements for the party.

23.____

24. A. Today, more then ever, we need the steadying influence of stable homes and families.
    B. Was ever a man so tormented!
    C. This report — may it never be forgotten — is our last, our very last.
    D. The letter states, "I am agin(sic) every idea you have."

24.____

25. A. Although he must have known the answer, he refused to volunteer the information.
    B. The pirate captain divided up the booty among his crew according to their rank.
    C. As the gale gathered force, the captain mounted the bridge.
    D. As he threw the line over the side of the boat, he suddenly remembered that the rope was fouled.

25.____

KEY (CORRECT ANSWERS)

1. B
2. D
3. A
4. C
5. D

6. A
7. C
8. D
9. B
10. D

11. A
12. D
13. A
14. B
15. B

16. B
17. A
18. B
19. C
20. A

21. C
22. B
23. D
24. A
25. B

PREPARING WRITTEN MATERIALS
EXAMINATION SECTION
TEST 1

DIRECTIONS: Each question or incomplete statement is followed by several suggested answers or completions. Select the one that BEST answers the question or completes the statement. *PRINT THE LETTER OF THE CORRECT ANSWER IN THE SPACE AT THE RIGHT.*

Questions 1-21.

DIRECTIONS: In each of the following sentences, which were taken from students' transcripts, there may be an error. Indicate the appropriate correction in the space at the right. If the sentence is correct as is, indicate this choice. Unnecessary changes will be considered incorrect.

1. In that building there seemed to be representatives of Teachers College, the Veterans Bureau, and the Businessmen's Association.
   A. Teacher's College
   B. Veterans' Bureau
   C. Businessmens Association
   D. Correct as is

   1.____

2. In his travels, he visited St. Paul, San Francisco, Springfield, Ohio, and Washington, D.C.
   A. Ohio and
   B. Saint Paul
   C. Washington, D.C.
   D. Correct as is

   2.____

3. As a result of their purchasing a controlling interest in the syndicate, it was well-known that the Bureau of Labor Statistics' calculations would be unimportant.
   A. of them purchasing
   B. well known
   C. Statistics
   D. Correct as is

   3.____

4. Walter Scott, Jr.'s, attempt to emulate his father's success was doomed to failure.
   A. Junior's,
   B. Scott's, Jr.
   C. Scott, Jr.'s attempt
   D. Correct as is

   4.____

5. About B.C. 250 the Romans invaded Great Britain, and remains of their highly developed civilization can still be seen.
   A. 250 B.C.
   Britain and
   C. highly-developed
   D. Correct as is

   5.____

6. The two boss's sons visited the children's department.
   A. bosses   B. bosses'   C. childrens'   D. Correct as is

   6.____

163

7. Miss Amex not only approved the report, but also decided that it needed no revision.
   A. report; but   B. report but   C. report. But   D. Correct as is

8. Here's brain food in a jiffy—economical, too!
   A. economical too!
   B. "brain food"
   C. jiffy-economical
   D. Correct as is

9. She said, "He likes the "Gatsby Look" very much."
   A. said "He
   B. "he
   C. 'Gatsby Look'
   D. Correct as is

10. We anticipate that we will be able to visit them briefly in Los Angeles on Wednesday after a five day visit.
    A. Wednes-   B. 5 day   C. five-day   D. Correct as is

11. She passed all her tests, and, she now has a good position.
    A. tests, and she
    B. past
    C. tests;
    D. Correct as is

12. The billing clerk said, "I will send the bill today"; however, that was a week ago, and it hasn't arrived yet!
    A. today;"   B. today,"   C. ago and   D. Correct as is

13. "She types at more-than-average speed," Miss Smith said, "but I feel that it is a result of marvelous concentration and self control on her part."
    A. more than average
    B. "But
    C. self-control
    D. Correct as is

14. The state of Alaska, the largest state in the union, is also the northernmost state.
    A. Union
    B. Northernmost State
    C. State of Alaska
    D. Correct as is

15. The memoirs of Ex-President Nixon, according to figures, sold more copies than Six Crises, the book he wrote in the '60s.
    A. Six Crises
    B. ex-President
    C. 60s
    D. Correct as is

16. "There are three principal elements, determining the hazard of buildings: the contents hazard, the fire resistance of the structure, and the character of the interior finish," concluded the speaker.
    The one of the following statements that is MOST acceptable is that, in the above passage,
    A. the comma following the word *elements* is incorrect
    B. the colon following the word *buildings* is incorrect
    C. the comma following the word *finish* is incorrect
    D. there is no error in the punctuation of the sentence

17. He spoke on his favorite topic, "Why We Will Win." (How could I stop him?)   17.____
    A. Win".   B. him?).   C. him)?   C. Correct as is

18. "All any insurance policy is, is a contract for services," said my insurance   18.____
    agent, Mr. Newton.
    A. Insurance Policy   B. Insurance Agent
    C. policy is is a   D. Correct as is

19. Inasmuch as the price list has now been up dated, we should sent it to the   19.____
    printer.
    A. In as much   B. updated
    C. pricelist   D. Correct as is

20. We feel that "Our know-how" is responsible for the improvement in technical   20.____
    developments.
    A. "our   B. know how   C. that,   D. Correct as is

21. Did Cortez conquer the Incas? the Aztecs? the South American Indians?   21.____
    A. Incas, the Aztecs, the South American Indians?
    B. Incas; the Aztecs; the South American Indians?
    C. south American Indians?
    D. Correct as is

22. Which one of the following forms for the typed name of the dictator in the closing   22.____
    lines of a letter is generally MOST acceptable in the United States?
    A. (Dr.) James F. Farley   B. Dr. James F. Farley
    C. Me. James J. Farley, Ph.D.   D. James F. Farley

23. The plural of   23.____
    A. turkey is turkies   B. cargo is cargoes
    C. bankruptcy is bankruptcys D. son-in-law is son-in-laws

24. The abbreviation viz. means MOST NEARLY   24.____
    A. namely   B. for example
    C. the following   D. see

25. In the sentence, *A man in a light-gray suit waited thirty-five minutes in the*   25.____
    ante-room for the all-important document, the word IMPROPERLY hyphenated
    is
    A. light-gray   B. thirty-five   C. ante-room   D. all-important

KEY (CORRECT ANSWERS)

1.	D	11.	A
2.	C	12.	D
3.	B	13.	D
4.	D	14.	A
5.	A	15.	B
6.	B	16.	A
7.	B	17.	D
8.	D	18.	D
9.	C	19.	B
10.	C	20.	A

21.	D
22.	D
23.	B
24.	A
25.	C

TEST 2

DIRECTIONS: Each question or incomplete statement is followed by several suggested answers or completions. Select the one that BEST answers the question or completes the statement. *PRINT THE LETTER OF THE CORRECT ANSWER IN THE SPACE AT THE RIGHT.*

Questions 1-10.

DIRECTIONS: In each of the following groups of four sentences, one sentence contains an error in sentence structure, grammar, usage, diction, or punctuation. Indicate the INCORRECT sentence.

1.
   A. The lecture finished, the audience began asking questions.
   B. Any man who could accomplish that task the world would regard as a hero.
   C. Our respect and admiration are mutual.
   D. George did like his mother told him, despite the importunities of his playmates.

   1._____

2.
   A. I cannot but help admiring you for your dedication to your job.
   B. Because they had insisted upon showing us films of their travels, we have lost many friends whom we once cherished.
   C. I am constrained to admit that your remarks made me feel bad.
   D. My brother having been notified of his acceptance by the university of his choice, my father immediately made plans for a vacation.

   2._____

3.
   A. In no other country is freedom of speech and assembly so jealously guarded.
   B. Being a beatnik, he felt that it would be a betrayal of his cause to wear shoes and socks at the same time.
   C. Riding over the Brooklyn Bridge gave us an opportunity to see the Manhattan skyline.
   D. In 1961, flaunting SEATO, the North Vietnamese crossed the line of demarcation.

   3._____

4.
   A. I have enjoyed the study of the Spanish language not only because of its beauty and the opportunity it offers to understand the Hispanic culture but also to make use of it in the business associations I have in South America.
   B. The opinions he expressed were decidedly different from those he had held in his youth.
   C. Had he actually studied, he certainly would have passed.
   D. A supervisor should be patient, tactful, and firm.

   4._____

5.
   A. At this point we were faced with only three alternatives: to push on, to remain where we were, or to return to the village.
   B. We had no choice but to forgive so venial a sin.
   C. In their new picture, the Warners are flouting tradition.
   D. Photographs taken revealed that 2.5 square miles had been burned.

   5._____

6. A. He asked whether he might write to his friends. 6.____
    B. There are many problems which must be solved before we can be assured of world peace.
    C. Each person with whom I talked expressed his opinion freely.
    D. Holding on to my saddle with all my strength the horse galloped down the road at a terrifying pace.

7. A. After graduating high school, he obtained a position as a runner in Wall Street. 7.____
    B. Last night, in a radio address, the President urged us to subscribe to the Red Cross.
    C. In the evening, light spring rain cooled the streets.
    D. "Un-American" is a word which has been used even by those whose sympathies may well have been pro-Nazi.

8. A. It is hard to conceive of their not doing good work. 8.____
    B. Who won—you or I?
    C. He having read the speech caused much comment.
    D. Their finishing the work proves that it can be done.

9. A. Our course of study should not be different now than it was five years ago. 9.____
    B. I cannot deny myself the pleasure of publicly thanking the mayor for his actions.
    C. The article on "Morale" has appeared in the Times Literary Supplement.
    D. He died of tuberculosis contracted during service with the Allied Forces.

10. A. If it wasn't for a lucky accident, he would still be an office-clerk. 10.____
    B. It is evident that teachers need help.
    C. Rolls of postage stamps may be bought at stationery stores.
    D. Addressing machines are used by firms that publish magazines.

11. The one of the following sentences which contains NO error in usage is: 11.____
    A. After the robbers left, the proprietor stood tied in his chair for about two hours before help arrived.
    B. In the cellar I found the watchmans' hat and coat.
    C. The persons living in adjacent apartments stated that they had heard no unusual noises.
    D. Neither a knife or any firearms were found in the room.

12. The one of the following sentences which contains NO error in usage is: 12.____
    A. The policeman lay a firm hand on the suspect's shoulder.
    B. It is true that neither strength nor agility are the most important requirement for a good patrolman.
    C. Good citizens constantly strive to do more than merely comply the restraints imposed by society.
    D. Twenty years is considered a severe sentence for a felony.

13. Select the sentence containing an adverbial objective.
    A. Concepts can only acquire content when they are connected, however indirectly, with sensible experience.
    B. The cloth was several shades too light to match the skirt which she had discarded.
    C. The Gargantuan Hall of Commons became a tri-daily horror to Kurt, because two youths discerned that he had a beard and courageously told the world about it.
    D. Brooding morbidly over the event, Elsie found herself incapable of engaging in normal activity.

14. Select the sentence containing a verb in the subjunctive mood.
    A. Had he known of the new experiments with penicillin dust for the cure of colds, he might have been tempted to try them in his own office.
    B. I should be very much honored by your visit.
    C. Though he has one of the highest intelligence quotients in his group, he seems far below the average in actual achievement.
    D. Long had I known that he would be the man finally selected for such signal honors.

15. Select the sentence containing one (or more) passive perfect participle(s).
    A. Having been apprised of the consequences of his refusal to answer, the witness finally revealed the source of his information.
    B. To have been placed in such an uncomfortable position was perhaps unfair to a journalist of his reputation.
    C. When deprived of special immunity he had, of course, no alternative but to speak.
    D. Having been obdurate until now, he was reluctant to surrender under this final pressure exerted upon him.

16. Select the sentence containing a predicate nominative.
    A. His dying wish, which he expressed almost with his last breath, was to see that justice was done toward his estranged wife.
    B. So long as we continue to elect our officials in truly democratic fashion, we shall have the power to preserve our liberties.
    C. We could do nothing, at this juncture, but walk the five miles back to camp.
    D. There was the spaniel, wet and cold and miserable, waiting silently at the door.

17. Select the sentence containing exactly TWO adverbs.
    A. The gentlemen advanced with exasperating deliberateness, while his lonely partner waited.
    B. If you are well, will you come early?
    C. I think you have guessed right, though you were rather slow, I must say.
    D. The last hundred years have seen more change than a thousand years of the Roman Empire, than a hundred thousand years of the stone age.

Questions 18-24.

DIRECTIONS: Select the choice describing the error in the sentence.

18. If us seniors do not support school functions, who will?
    A. Unnecessary shift in tense
    B. Incomplete sentence
    C. Improper case of pronoun
    D. Lack of parallelism

19. The principal has issued regulations which, in my opinion, I think are too harsh.
    A. Incorrect punctuation
    B. Faulty sentence structure
    C. Misspelling
    D. Redundant expression

20. The freshmens' and sophomores' performances equaled those of the juniors and seniors.
    A. Ambiguous reference
    B. Incorrect placement of punctuation
    C. Misspelling of past tense
    D. Incomplete comparison

21. Each of them, Anne and her, is an outstanding pianist I can't tell you which one is best.
    A. Lack of agreement
    B. Improper degree of comparison
    C. Incorrect case of pronoun
    D. Run-on sentence

22. She wears clothes that are more expensive than my other friends.
    A. Misuse of *than*
    B. Incorrect relative pronoun
    C. Shift in tense
    D. Faulty comparison

23. At the very end of the story it implies that the children's father died tragically.
    A. Misuse of *implies*
    B. Indefinite use of pronoun
    C. Incorrect spelling
    D. Incorrect possessive

24. At the end of the game both of us, John and me, couldn't scarcely walk because we were so tired.
    A. Incorrect punctuation
    B. Run-on sentence
    C. Incorrect case of pronoun
    D. Double negative

Questions 25-30.

DIRECTIONS: Questions 25 through 30 consist of a sentence lacking certain needed punctuation. Pick as your answer the description of punctuation which will CORRECTLY complete the sentence.

25. If you take the time to keep up your daily correspondence you will no doubt be most efficient.
    A. Comma only after *doubt*
    B. Comma only after *correspondence*
    C. Commas after *correspondence*, *will*, and *be*
    D. Commas after *if*, *correspondence*, and *will*

26. Because he did not send the application soon enough he did not receive the up to date copy of the book.
    A. Commas after *application* and *enough*, and quotation marks before *up* and after *date*
    B. Commas after *application* and *enough*, and hyphens between *to* and *date*
    C. Comma after *enough*, and hyphens between *up* and *to* and between *to* and *date*
    D. Comma after *application*, and quotation marks before *up* and after *date*

27. The coordinator requested from the department the following items a letter each week summarizing progress personal forms and completed applications for tests.
    A. Commas after *items* and *completed*
    B. Semi-colon after *items* and *progress*, comma after *forms*
    C. Colon after *items*, commas after *progress* and *forms*
    D. Colon after *items*, commas after *forms* and *applications*

28. The supervisor asked Who will attend the conference next month.
    A. Comma after *asked*, period after *month*
    B. Period after *asked*, question mark after *month*
    C. Comma after *asked*, quotation marks before *Who*, quotation marks after *month*, and question mark after the quotation marks
    D. Comma after *asked*, quotation marks before *Who*, question mark after *month*, and quotation marks after the question mark

29. When the statistics are collected, we will forward the results to you as soon as possible.
    A. Comma after *you*
    B. Commas after *forward* and *you*
    C. Commas after *collected*, *results* and *you*
    D. Comma after *collected*

30. The ecology of our environment is concerned with mans pollution of the atmosphere.
    A. Comma after *ecology*
    B. Apostrophe after *n* and before *s* in *mans*
    C. Commas after *ecology* and *environment*
    D. Apostrophe after *s* in *mans*

KEY (CORRECT ANSWERS)

1.	D	11.	C	21.	B
2.	A	12.	D	22.	D
3.	D	13.	B	23.	B
4.	A	14.	A	24.	D
5.	B	15.	A	25.	B
6.	D	16.	A	26.	C
7.	A	17.	C	27.	C
8.	C	18.	C	28.	D
9.	A	19.	D	29.	D
10.	A	20.	B	30.	B

TEST 3

DIRECTIONS: Each question or incomplete statement is followed by several suggested answers or completions. Select the one that BEST answers the question or completes the statement. *PRINT THE LETTER OF THE CORRECT ANSWER IN THE SPACE AT THE RIGHT.*

Questions 1-6.

DIRECTIONS: From the four choices offered in Questions 1 through 6, select the one which is INCORRECT.

1.
   A. Before we try to extricate ourselves from this struggle in which we are now engaged in, we must be sure that we are not severing ties of honor and duty.
   B. Besides being an outstanding student, he is also a leader in school government and a trophy-winner in school sports.
   C. If the framers of the Constitution were to return to life for a day, their opinion of our amendments would be interesting.
   D. Since there are three m's in the word, it is frequently misspelled.

   1.____

2.
   A. It was a college with an excellance beyond question.
   B. The coach will accompany the winners, whomever they may be.
   C. The dean, together with some other faculty members, is planning a conference.
   D. The jury are arguing among themselves.

   2.____

3.
   A. This box is less nearly square than that one.
   B. Wagner is many persons' choice as the world's greatest composer.
   C. The habits of Copperheads are different from Diamond Backs.
   D. The teacher maintains that the child was insolent.

   3.____

4.
   A. There was a time when the Far North was unknown territory. Now American soldiers manning radar stations there wave to Boeing jet planes zooming by overhead.
   B. Exodus, the psalms, and Deuteronomy are all books of the Old Testament.
   C. Linda identified her china dishes by marking their bottoms with india ink.
   D. Harry S. Truman, former president of the United States, served as a captain in the American army during World War I.

   4.____

5.
   A. The sequel of their marriage was a divorce.
   B. We bought our car secondhand.
   C. His whereabouts is unknown.
   D. Jones offered to use his own car, providing the company would pay for gasoline, oil, and repairs,

   5.____

6. A. I read Golding's "Lord of the Flies". 6.____
   B. The orator at the civil rights rally thrilled the audience when he said, "I quote Robert Burns's line, 'A man's a man for a' that.'"
   C. The phrase "producer to consumer" is commonly used by market analysts.
   D. The lawyer shouted, "Is not this evidence illegal?"

Questions 7-9.

DIRECTIONS: In answering Questions 7 through 9, mark the letter A if faulty because of incorrect grammar, mark the letter B if faulty because of incorrect punctuation, mark the letter C if correct.

7. Mr. Brown our accountant, will audit the accounts next week. 7.____

8. Give the assignment to whomever is able to do it most efficiently. 8.____

9. The supervisor expected either your or I to file these reports. 9.____

Questions 10-14.

DIRECTIONS: In each of the following groups of four sentences, one sentence contains an error in sentence structure, grammar, usage, diction, or punctuation. Indicate the INCORRECT sentence.

10. A. The agent asked, "Did you say, 'Never again?'" 10.____
    B. Kindly let me know whether you can visit us on the 17th.
    C. "I cannot accept that!" he exploded. "Please show me something else.
    D. Ed, will you please lend me your grass shears for an hour or so.

11. A. Recalcitrant though he may have been, Alexander was willfully destructive. 11.____
    B. Everybody should look out for himself.
    C. John is one of those students who usually spends most of his time in the principal's office.
    D. She seems to feel that what is theirs is hers.

12. A. Be he ever so much in the wrong, I'll support the man while deploring his actions. 12.____
    B. The schools' lack of interest in consumer education is shortsighted.
    C. I think that Fitzgerald's finest stanza is one which includes the reference to youth's "sweet-scented manuscript.
    D. I never would agree to Anderson having full control of the company's policies.

13. A. We had to walk about five miles before finding a gas station. 13.____
    B. The willful sending of a false alarm has, and may, result in homicide.
    C. Please bring that book to me at once.
    D. Neither my sister nor I am interested in bowling.

14. A. He is one of the very few football players who doesn't wear a helmet with a face guard.
    B. But three volunteers appeared at the recruiting office.
    C. Such consideration as you can give us will be appreciated.
    D. When I left them, the group were disagreeing about the proposed legislation.

14.____

Question 15.

DIRECTIONS: Question 15 contains two sentences concerning criminal law. The sentences could contain errors in English grammar or usage. A sentence does not contain an error simply because it could be written in a different manner. In answering this question, choose answer
A. if only sentence I is correct
B. if only sentence II is correct
C. if both sentences are correct
D. if neither sentence is correct

15. I. The use of fire or explosives to destroy tangible property is proscribed by the criminal mischief provisions of the Revised Penal Law.
    II. The defendant's taking of a taxicab for the immediate purpose of affecting his escape did not constitute grand larceny.

15.____

KEY (CORRECT ANSWERS)

1.	A	6.	A	11.	C
2.	B	7.	B	12.	D
3.	C	8.	A	13.	B
4.	B	9.	A	14.	A
5.	D	10	A	15.	A

PREPARING WRITTEN MATERIALS
EXAMINATION SECTION
TEST 1

DIRECTIONS: Each question contains a sentence. Read each sentence carefully to decide whether it is correct. Then, in the space at the right, mark your answer:
- A. If the sentence is incorrect because of bad grammar or sentence structure;
- B. If the sentence is incorrect because of bad punctuation
- C. If the sentence is incorrect because of bad capitalization
- D. If the sentence is correct.

Each incorrect sentence has only one type of error. Consider a sentence correct if it has no errors, although there may be other correct ways of saying the same thing.

SAMPLE QUESTION I: One of our clerks were promoted yesterday.

The subject of this sentence is *one*, so the verb should be *was promoted* instead of *were promoted*. Since the sentence is incorrect because of bad grammar, the answer to Sample Question I is A.

SAMPLE QUESTION II: Between you and me, I would prefer not going there.

Since this sentence is correct, the answer to Sample Question II is D.

1. The National alliance of Businessmen is trying to persuade private businesses to hire youth in the summertime. 1.____

2. The supervisor who is on vacation, is in charge of processing vouchers. 2.____

3. The activity of the committee at its conferences is always stimulating. 3.____

4. After checking the addresses again, the letters went to the mailroom. 4.____

5. The director, as well as the employees, are interested in sharing the dividends. 5.____

6. The experiments conducted by professor Alford were described at a recent meeting of our organization. 6.____

7. I shall be glad to discuss these matters with whoever represents the Municipal Credit Union. 7.____

8. In my opinion, neither Mr. Price nor Mr. Roth knows how to operate this office appliance. 8.____

9. The supervisor, as well as the other stenographers, were unable to transcribe Miss Johnson's shorthand notes.

10. Important functions such as, recruiting and training, are performed by our unit.

11. Realizing that many students are interested in this position, we sent announcements to all the High Schools.

12. After pointing out certain incorrect conclusions, the report was revised by Mr. Clark and submitted to Mr. Batson.

13. The employer contributed two hundred dollars; the employees, one hundred dollars.

14. He realized that the time, when a supervisor could hire and fire, was over.

15. The complaints received by Commissioner Regan was the cause of the change in policy.

16. Any report, that is to be sent to the Federal Security Administration, must be approved and signed by Mr. Yound.

17. Of the two stenographers, Miss Rand is the more accurate.

18. Since the golf courses are crowded during the summer, more men are needed to maintain the courses in good playing condition.

19. Although he invited Mr. Frankel and I to attend a meeting of the Civil Service Assembly, we were unable to accept his invitation.

20. Only the employees who worked overtime last week may leave one hour earlier today.

21. We need someone who can speak french fluently.

22. A tall, elderly, man entered the office and asked to see Mr. Brown.

23. The clerk insisted that he had filed the correspondence in the proper cabinet.

24. "Will you assist us," he asked?

25. According to the information contained in the report, a large quantity of paper and envelopes were used by this bureau last year.

KEY (CORRECT ANSWERS)

1.	C	11.	C
2.	B	12.	A
3.	D	13.	D
4.	A	14.	B
5.	A	15.	A
6.	C	16.	B
7.	D	17.	D
8.	D	18.	C
9.	A	19.	A
10.	B	20.	D

21. C
22. B
23. D
24. B
25. A

TEST 2

DIRECTIONS: Each question consists of a sentence which may be classified appropriately under one of the following four categories:
    A. Incorrect because of faulty grammar or sentence structure.
    B. Incorrect because of faulty punctuation.
    C. Incorrect because of faulty capitalization.
    D. Correct

Examine each sentence carefully. Then, in the space at the right, print the capital letter preceding the option which is the BEST of the four suggested above. All incorrect sentences contain only one type of error. Consider a sentence correct if it contains none of the types of errors mentioned, although there may be other correct ways of expressing the same thought.

1. Mrs. Black the supervisor of the unit, has many important duties.   1.____
2. We spoke to the man whom you saw yesterday.   2.____
3. When a holiday falls on sunday, it is officially celebrated on monday.   3.____
4. Of the two reports submitted, this one is the best.   4.____
5. Each staff member, including the accountants, were invited to the meeting.   5.____
6. Give the package to whomever calls for it.   6.____
7. To plan the work is our responsibility; to carry it out is his.   7.____
8. "May I see the person in charge of this office," asked the visitor?   8.____
9. He knows that it was not us who prepared the report.   9.____
10. These problems were brought to the attention of senator Johnson.   10.____
11. The librarian classifies all books periodicals and documents.   11.____
12. Any employee who uses an adding machine realizes its importance.   12.____
13. Instead of coming to the office, the clerk should of come to the supply room.   13.____
14. He asked, "will your staff assist us?"   14.____
15. Having been posted on the bulletin board, we were certain that the announcements would be read.   15.____
16. He was not informed, that he would have to work overtime.   16.____
17. The wind blew several paper off of his desk.   17.____

18. Charles Dole, who is a member of the committee, was asked to confer with commissioner Wilson.   18.____

19. Miss Bell will issue a copy to whomever asks for one.   19.____

20. Most employees, and he is no exception do not like to work overtime.   20.____

21. This is the man whom you interviewed last week.   21.____

22. Of the two cities visited, White Plains is the cleanest.   22.____

23. Although he was willing to work on other holidays, he refused to work on Labor day.   23.____

24. If an employee wishes to attend the conference, he should fill out the necessary forms.   24.____

25. The division chief reports that an engineer and an inspector is needed for this special survey.   25.____

KEY (CORRECT ANSWERS)

1.	B	11.	B
2.	D	12.	D
3.	C	13.	A
4.	A	14.	C
5.	A	15.	A
6.	A	16.	B
7.	D	17.	A
8.	B	18.	C
9.	A	19.	A
10.	C	20.	B

21. D
22. A
23. C
24. D
25. A

TEST 3

DIRECTIONS: Each question consists of a sentence which may be classified appropriately under one of the following four categories:
- A. Incorrect because of faulty grammar or sentence structure.
- B. Incorrect because of faulty punctuation.
- C. Incorrect because of faulty capitalization.
- D. Correct

Examine each sentence carefully. Then, in the space at the right, print the capital letter preceding the option which is the BEST of the four suggested above. All incorrect sentences contain only one type of error. Consider a sentence correct if it contains none of the types of errors mentioned, although there may be other correct ways of expressing the same thought.

1. We have learned that there was more than twelve people present at the meeting. 1._____

2. Every one of the employees is able to do this kind of work. 2._____

3. Neither the supervisor nor his assistant are in the office today. 3._____

4. The office manager announced that any clerk, who volunteered for the assignment, would be rewarded. 4._____

5. After looking carefully in all the files, the letter was finally found on a desk. 5._____

6. In answer to the clerk's question, the supervisor said, "this assignment must be completed today." 6._____

7. The office manager says that he can permit only you and me to go to the meeting. 7._____

8. The supervisor refused to state who he would assign to the reception unit. 8._____

9. At the last meeting, he said that he would interview us in september. 9._____

10. Mr. Jones, who is one of our most experienced employees has been placed in charge of the main office. 10._____

11. I think that this adding machine is the most useful of the two we have in our office. 11._____

12. Between you and I, our new stenographer is not as competent as our former stenographer. 12._____

13. The new assignment should be given to whoever can do the work rapidly 13._____

14. Mrs. Smith, as well as three other typists, was assigned to the new office. 14._____

15. The staff assembled for the conference on time but, the main speaker arrived late. 15.____

16. The work was assigned to Miss Green and me. 16.____

17. The staff regulations state that an employee, who is frequently tardy, may receive a negative evaluation. 17.____

18. He is the kind of person who is always willing to undertake difficult assignments. 18.____

19. Mr. Wright's request cannot be granted under no conditions. 19.____

20. George Colt a new employee, was asked to deliver the report to the Domestic Relations Court. 20.____

21. The supervisor entered the room and said, "The work must be completed today." 21.____

22. The employees were given their assignments and, they were asked to begin work immediately. 22.____

23. The letter will be sent to the United States senate this week. 23.____

24. When the supervisor entered the room, he noticed that the book was laying on the desk. 24.____

25. The price of the pens were higher than the price of the pencils. 25.____

KEY (CORRECT ANSWERS)

1.	A	11.	A
2.	D	12.	A
3.	A	13.	D
4.	B	14.	D
5.	A	15.	B
6.	C	16.	D
7.	D	17.	B
8.	A	18.	D
9.	C	19.	A
10.	B	20.	B

21. D
22. B
23. C
24. A
25. A

RECORD KEEPING
EXAMINATION SECTION
TEST 1

DIRECTIONS: Each question or incomplete statement is followed by several suggested answers or completions. Select the one that BEST answers the question or completes the statement. *PRINT THE LETTER OF THE CORRECT ANSWER IN THE SPACE AT THE RIGHT.*

Questions 1-15.

DIRECTIONS: Questions 1 through 15 are to be answered on the basis of the following list of company names below. Arrange a file alphabetically, word-by-word, disregarding punctuation, conjunctions, and apostrophes. Then answer the questions.

    A Bee C Reading Materials
    ABCO Parts
    A Better Course for Test Preparation
    AAA Auto Parts Co.
    A-Z Auto Parts, Inc.
    Aabar Books
    Abbey, Joanne
    Boman-Sylvan Law Firm
    BMW Autowerks
    C Q Service Company
    Chappell-Murray, Inc.
    E&E Life Insurance
    Emcrisco
    Gigi Arts
    Gordon, Jon & Associates
    SOS Plumbing
    Schmidt, J.B. Co.

1. Which of these files should appear FIRST?
    A. ABCO Parts
    B. A Bee C Reading Materials
    C. A Better Course for Test Preparation
    D. AAA Auto Parts Co.

2. Which of these files should appear SECOND?
    A. A-Z Auto Parts, Inc.
    B. A Bee C Reading Materials
    C. A Better Course for Test Preparation
    D. AAA Auto Parts Co.

2 (#1)

3. Which of these files should appear THIRD? 3.____
   A. ABCO Parts B. A Bee C Reading Materials
   C. Aabar Books D. AAA Auto Parts Co.

4. Which of these files should appear FOURTH? 4.____
   A. Aabar Books B. ABCO Parts
   C. Abbey, Joanne D. AAA Auto Parts Co.

5. Which of these files should appear LAST? 5.____
   A. Gordon, Jon & Associates B. Gigi Arts
   C. Schmidt, J.B. Co. D. SOS Plumbing

6. Which of these files should appear between A-Z Auto Parts, Inc. and Abbey, 6.____
   Joanne?
   A. A Bee C Reading Materials
   B. AAA Auto Parts Co.
   C. ABCO Parts
   D. A Better Course for Test Preparation

7. Which of these files should appear between ABCO Parts and Aabar Books? 7.____
   A. A Bee C Reading Materials B. Abbey, Joanne
   C. Aabar Books D. A-Z Auto Parts

8. Which of these files should appear between Abbey, Joanne and Boman-Sylvan 8.____
   Law Firm?
   A. A Better Course for Test Preparation
   B. BMW Autowerks
   C. Chappell-Murray, Inc.
   D. Aabar Books

9. Which of these files should appear between Abbey, Joanne and C Q Service? 9.____
   A. A-Z Auto Parts, Inc. B. BMW Autowerks
   C. Choices A and B D. Chappell-Murray, Inc.

10. Which of these files should appear between C Q Service Company and 10.____
    Emcrisco?
    A. Chappell-Murray, Inc. B. E&E Life Insurance
    C. Gigi Arts D. Choices A and B

11. Which of these files should NOT appear between C Q Service Company and 11.____
    E&E Life Insurance?
    A. Gordon, Jon & Associates B. Emcrisco
    C. Gigi Arts D. All of the above

12. Which of these files should appear between Chappell-Murray, Inc. and Gigi Arts? 12.____
    A. C Q Service Inc., E&E Life Insurance, and Emcrisco
    B. Emcrisco, E&E Life Insurance, and Gordon, Jon & Associates
    C. E&E Life Insurance, and Emcrisco
    D. Emcrisco and Gordon, Jon & Associates

13. Which of these files should appear between Gordon, Jon & Associates and SOS Plumbing? 13.____
    A. Gigi Arts
    B. Schmidt, J.B. Co.
    C. Choices A and B
    D. None of the above

14. Each of the choices lists the four files in their proper alphabetical order EXCEPT 14.____
    A. E&E Life Insurance; Gigi Arts; Gordon, Jon & Associates; SOS Plumbing
    B. E&E Life Insurance; Emcrisco; Gigi Arts; SOS Plumbing
    C. Emcrisco; Gordon, Jon & Associates; SOS Plumbing; Schmidt, J.B. Co.
    D. Emcrisco; Gigi Arts; Gordon, Jon & Associates; SOS Plumbing

15. Which of the choices lists the four files in their proper alphabetical order? 15.____
    A. Gigi Arts; Gordon, Jon & Associates; SOS Plumbing; Schmidt, J.B. Co.
    B. Gordon, Jon & Associates; Gigi Arts; Schmidt, J.B. Co.; SOS Plumbing
    C. Gordon, Jon & Associates; Gigi Arts; SOS Plumbing; Schmidt, J.B. Co.
    D. Gigi Arts; Gordon, Jon & Associates; Schmidt, J.B. Co.; SOS Plumbing

16. The alphabetical filing order of two businesses with identical names is determined by the 16.____
    A. length of time each business has been operating
    B. addresses of the businesses
    C. last name of the company president
    D. no one of the above

17. In an alphabetical filing system, if a business name includes a number, it should be 17.____
    A. disregarded
    B. considered a number and placed at the end of an alphabetical section
    C. treated as though it were written in words and alphabetized accordingly
    D. considered a number and placed at the beginning of an alphabetical section

18. If a business name includes a contraction (such as *don't* or *it's*), how should that word be treated in an alphabetical system? 18.____
    A. Divide the word into its separate parts and treat it as two words
    B. Ignore the letters that come after the apostrophe
    C. Ignore the word that contains the contraction
    D. Ignore the apostrophe and consider all letters in the contraction

19. In what order should the parts of an address be considered when using an alphabetical filing system?   19._____
    A. City or town; state; street name; house or building number
    B. State; city or town; street name; house or building number
    C. House or building number; street name; city or town; state
    D. Street name; city or town; state

20. A business record should be cross-referenced when a(n)   20._____
    A. organization is known by an abbreviated name
    B. business has a name change because of a sale, incorporation, or other reason
    C. business is known by a *coined* or common name which differs from a dictionary spelling
    D. all of the above

21. A geographical filing system is MOST effective when   21._____
    A. location is more important than name
    B. many names or titles sound alike
    C. dealing with companies who have offices all over the world
    D. filing personal and business files

Questions 22-25.

DIRECTIONS: Questions 22 through 25 are to be answered on the basis of the list of items below, which are to be filed geographically. Organize the items geographically and then answer the questions.

    I.   University Press at Berkeley, U.S.
    II. Maria Sanchez, Mexico City, Mexico
    III. Great Expectations Ltd. in London, England
    IV. Justice League, Cape Town, South Africa, Africa
    V.   Crown Pearls Ltd. in London, England
    VI. Joseph Prasad in London, England

22. Which of the following arrangements of the items is composed according to the policy of: *Continent, Country, City, Firm or Individual Name*?   22._____
    A. V, III, IV, VI, II, I   B. IV, V, III, VI, II, I
    C. I, IV, V, III, VI, II   D. IV, V, III, VI, I, II

23. Which of the following files is arranged according to the policy of: 23._____
    Continent, Country, City, Firm or Individual Name?
    A. South Africa; Africa; Cape Town; Justice League
    B. Mexico; Mexico City; Maria Sanchez
    C. North America; United States; Berkeley; University Press
    D. England; Europe; London; Prasad, Joseph

5 (#1)

24. Which of the following arrangements of the items is composed according to the policy of: *Country, City, Firm or Individual Name*?   24.____
    A. V, VI, III, II, IV, I
    B. I, V, VI, III, II, IV
    C. VI, V, III, II, IV, I
    D. V, III, VI, II, IV, I

25. Which of the following files is arranged according to a policy of: *Country, City, Firm or Individual Name*?   25.____
    A. England; London; Crown Pearls Ltd.
    B. North America; United States; Berkeley; University Press
    C. Africa; Cape Town; Justice League
    D. Mexico City; Mexico; Maria Sanchez

26. Under which of the following circumstances would a phonetic filing system be MOST effective?   26.____
    A. When the person in charge of filing can't spell very well
    B. With large files with names that sound alike
    C. With large files with names that are spelled alike
    D. All of the above

Questions 27-29.

DIRECTIONS: Questions 27 through 29 are to be answered on the basis of the following list of numerical files.

    I.   391-023-100
    II. 361-132-170
    III. 385-732-200
    IV. 381-432-150
    V.   391-632-387
    VI. 361-423-303
    VII. 391-123-271

27. Which of the following arrangements of the files follows a consecutive-digit system?   27.____
    A. II, III, IV, I   B. I, V, VII, III   C. II, IV, III, I   D. III, I, V, VII

28. Which of the following arrangements follows a terminal-digit system?   28.____
    A. I, VII, II, IV, III
    B. II, I, IV, V, VII
    C. VII, VI, V, IV, III
    D. I, IV, II, III, VII

29. Which of the following lists follows a middle-digit system?   29.____
    A. I, VII, II, VI, IV, V, III
    B. I, II, VII, IV, VI, V, III
    C. VII, II, I, III, V, VI, IV
    D. VII, I, II, IV, VI, V, III

Questions 30-31.

DIRECTIONS: Questions 30 and 31 are to be answered on the basis of the following information.

  I. Reconfirm Laura Bates appointment with James Caldecort on December 12 at 9:30 A.M.
  II. Laurence Kinder contact Julia Lucas on August 3 and set up a meeting for week of September 23 at 4 P.M.
  III. John Lutz contact Larry Waverly on August 3 and set up appointment for September 23 at 9:30 A.M.
  IV. Call for tickets for Gerry Stanton August 21 for New Jersey on September 23, flight 143 at 4:43 P.M.

30. A chronological file for the above information would be 30.____
    A. IV, III, II, I   B. III, II, IV, I   C. IV, II, III, I   D. III, I, II, IV

31. Using the above information, a chronological file for the date September 23 would be 31.____
    A. II, III, IV   B. III, I, IV   C. III, II, IV   D. IV, III, II

Questions 32-34.

DIRECTIONS: Questions 32 through 34 are to be answered on the basis of the following information.

  I. Call Roger Epstein, Ashoke Naipaul, Jon Anderson, and Sara Washingon on April 19 at 1:00 P.M. to set up meeting with Alika D'Ornay for June 6 in New York.
  II. Call Martin Ames before noon on April 19 to confirm afternoon meeting with Bob Greenwood on April 20th.
  III. Set up meeting room at noon for 2:30 P.M. meeting on April 19th.
  IV. Ashley Stanton contact Bob Greenwood at 9:00 A.M. on April 20 and set up meeting for June 6 at 8:30 A.M.
  V. Carol Guiland contact Shelby Van Ness during afternoon of April 20 and set up meeting for June 6 at 10:00 A.M.
  VI. Call airline and reserve tickets on June 6 for Roger Epstein trip to Denver on July 8.
  VII. Meeting at 2:30 P.M. on April 19th.

32. A chronological file for all of the above information would be 32.____
    A. II, I, III, VII, V, IV, VI   B. III, VII, II, I, IV, V, VI
    C. III, VII, I, II, V, IV, VI   D. II, III, I, VII, IV, V, VI

33. A chronological file for the date of April 19th would be 33.____
    A. II, III, VII, I   B. II, III, I, VII   C. VII, I, III, II   D. III, VII, I, II

34. Add the following information to the file, and then create a chronological file for April 20th: VIII. April 20: 3:00 P.M. meeting between Bob Greenwood and Martin Ames.   34.____
    A. IV, V, VIII   B. IV, VIII, V   C. VIII, V, IV   D. V, IV, VIII

35. The PRIMARY advantage of computer records over a manual system is   35.____
    A. speed of retrieval   B. accuracy
    C. cost   D. potential file loss

KEY (CORRECT ANSWERS)

1.	B	11.	D	21.	A	31.	C
2.	C	12.	C	22.	B	32.	D
3.	D	13.	B	23.	C	33.	B
4.	A	14.	C	24.	D	34.	A
5.	D	15.	D	25.	A	35.	A
6.	C	16.	B	26.	B		
7.	B	17.	C	27.	C		
8.	B	18.	D	28.	D		
9.	C	19.	A	29.	A		
10.	D	20.	D	30.	B		

www.ingramcontent.com/pod-product-compliance
Lightning Source LLC
Chambersburg PA
CBHW082039300426
44117CB00015B/2535